# THE
# FIVE STAR
# FORMULA

Create incredible guest experiences
that lead to five star reviews and
an award winning hospitality business

*Joy Zarine*

First published in Great Britain 2017
by Rethink Press (www.rethinkpress.com)

# CONTENTS

| | |
|---|---|
| Foreword | 7 |
| Introduction | 11 |

## SECTION ONE
## CLARITY — 15

| | |
|---|---|
| Chapter 1 | |
| Why Have a Five Star Business Anyway? | 17 |
| Chapter 2 | |
| What Is Your 'Why'? | 23 |
| Chapter 3 | |
| Understanding Your Business Better | 29 |
| Chapter 4 | |
| Your Mission and Your Vision | 37 |
|    Finding your mission | 39 |
|    Finding your vision | 40 |
| Chapter 5 | |
| Building Your Dream | 43 |
|    Culture | 44 |
|    Customer | 45 |
|    Creativity | 46 |

**SECTION TWO**
## CULTURE 49

Chapter 6
How to Catch Butterflies 51
  Grow a garden 56

Chapter 7
Leadership Is a Contact Sport 59

Chapter 8
Walking the Talk 65
  Training 68
  The daily huddle 68
  Quarterly one-to-ones 69

Chapter 9
Recognition 71
  Individual goals 74
  Team targets 74

Chapter 10
Set for Success 77

**SECTION THREE**
## CUSTOMERS 83

Chapter 11
Great Expectations 85
  Defining your 'perfect' guest 87
  Understanding guests' expectations 89
  How to attract your perfect guests 90

Chapter 12
Delivering The Dream    91
   Service standards    91
   Consistency is king    93
   Building systems    95

Chapter 13
The Extra Mile    97
   Indulge the senses    99
   Know your onions    101
   Surprise and delight    103
   Excel with technology    104

Chapter 14
The Everlasting Review    107

Chapter 15
Winning With Reviews    111

**SECTION FOUR**
**CREATIVITY**    **117**

Chapter 16
From 'Bland' To 'Brand'    119
   Be remarkable    121
   Take the risk    123

Chapter 17
Finding Your Unicorn    127

Chapter 18
Becoming The Talk Of The Town    131
   Influencing the influencer    134

Chapter 19
Partnerships                                    137

Chapter 20
Creating Fame                                   143

**SECTION FIVE**
**COMMENDATIONS**                               **149**

Chapter 21
The Power Of Awards                             151

Chapter 22
Being In It To Win It                           155

Chapter 23
Meet The Judges                                 161

Chapter 24
Telling The World                              165

Chapter 25
What Next?                                      169

Afterword                                       175
Acknowledgments                                 177
About The Author                                179

# FOREWORD

I first worked with Joy over ten years ago, when we were both managers for a small group of bars. Although we didn't work in the same bar, as a group of individuals we were very tight knit, always spending time together and bouncing ideas around. I was always envious of the bar she ran, how effortlessly they seemed to get the marketing right and how she built her business into a brand. We used to joke that I was an eggs and flour man, she was much more icing and cherry.

I felt I had a good grip on making my bar function and run smoothly, but if I'm honest, the details that really make the experience special could feel clumsy. Whether it was our social media message, the bookings through our website or what we did on our posters, I always found it really challenging to know what to do for the best. The crucial thing I know now was I was looking at it as marketing, rather than understanding the guest experience.

I know now that I didn't know the details in my business well enough. I didn't understand the guest experience, or my guests' expectations. I didn't know how to build systems so strong that you get it right every time. I was miles away from running a Five Star Business.

I had to learn to focus my energy on what matters, the details that make an experience, those tiny things that make your guests love what you do. You can have the best food, the most amazing drinks, even the most incredible service. However, there's no point in any of that if your guest can't book a table because the website doesn't function properly. Everything has to flow, and it all has to work together.

That's what I learnt from working with Joy.

Today I own an award-winning gourmet burger and cocktail restaurant in South East London called Hello Burger. Working with Joy has been some of the most enlightening, rewarding and downright fun I've had professionally. I am so pleased that she has put down her concepts and ideas here on paper, and so many people can benefit from them.

This book is not just about making more profits. Yes, of course you have to make money in your business, but this book is about the formula for creating a Five Star Business. One that is not just financially stable, but award-winning, has a great reputation and trades consistently for many years to come.

Going through this process is not easy. You still need to bring energy, ideas and passion to the table, but if you want to transform your bar or restaurant the answers are in this book. This book will not simply make you more money, it will help you to build a stronger, more robust business. This book unlocks how to have a Five Star Business that is clear about what it is (and what it isn't), that ultimately gives your guests a better experience.

I'll give you an example.

Bottomless Brunch has been been incredibly popular over recent years. It's no doubt a lot of fun, there's value in it for your guests, and it can make money. But in my restaurant, I choose not to do it and here is why. Imagine we could add 100 covers a week at £35 per head, why wouldn't you? I didn't because I want the product to be the hero of my business; which is a well thought out, amazing experience.

I feel like in the long run we would become less about having an amazing date night, a catch up with friends, family meal or whatever, and more about binge drinking. It starts to move away from what I have worked so hard to build. It's short term and gimmicky in my view. I'm not saying that Bottomless Brunch is bad, it may be perfect for your business. I felt it would begin to shift my business away from great food, cocktails and experience, and eventually that could cannibalise what we do.

It's hard to turn down £3,500 a week, right? It is, but I just felt that the families, for example, would just steer clear. That wouldn't just be for brunch either, it would change the reputation, change the focus of my business. That isn't a risk I'm prepared to take.

The hospitality industry is full of people who care deeply about what they do; unfortunately focus and energy is often directed in the wrong place. Gimmicks, offers, flooding Facebook with general interest – none of that dials in on what matters: your guest's experience. There comes a point where what you charge becomes far less important, and no matter how low your prices are, or how good your latest deal is, if it's not an amazing experience, you're going to struggle.

There is no way of knowing exactly what the future holds, but I do know there will be endless decisions on what is best for your business. It's staggering to think of the amount of times I have faced difficult decisions and simply thought about the guest experience. It gave me the answers time and again. It will set you apart from all of your competitors and leave you something special, and something that will last.

Good on you for picking this book up. It shows that you care, that you want your business to be better, I applaud that. In today's climate, you've got to be better, your guest experience has got to be better. Watching your business improve is just awesome, really special and wonderfully rewarding.

Good luck and enjoy the book.

**TONY ADAMS**
Hospitality industry expert and award-winning restaurateur

# INTRODUCTION

Do you dream of opening your own restaurant one day? Do you have ideas, but you're not really sure if you have it all figured out? Or perhaps you already own or manage a pub, restaurant, club or bar and you are running out of ideas on how to take your business to the next level. Are the bills never-ending and you find yourself caught up every day simply putting out fires in your business? Are days off spent dealing with issues from afar, so much so that you might as well have gone to work anyway? Do you hate the stress of having to deal with reviews and complaints? Do you realise there are improvements that need to be made within your business? If only you had the time to sit down and make a plan.

I hope *The Five Star Formula* will be the answer to your problems and the roadmap you need to transform your business.

So what makes me qualified to write this book? Well, the good news is this book is not about me and my business; instead, it is about you and yours. My successes and life experiences are only relevant to assure you that the advice I give is tried and tested across a multitude of restaurants, bars, pubs and hotels. You can, I hope, believe that your time will be well spent in reading and implementing what I have to say.

I have been fortunate enough to have found an industry that I fall more in love with every day. In my early career, I worked alongside a number of industry leaders, getting paid in roles where I simply had to make people happy. From bartending to hosting, event planning to managing, whatever role I was being paid to do, I was ultimately tasked with making my guests happy, and I thrived on that.

Over ten years ago, I launched my own consultancy, working one-to-one with an array of incredible venues from small independent restaurants to international hotel brands. The challenges have been relentless, but taking a business from the brink of bankruptcy, through the wilderness and ultimately on to prosperity makes my heart sing.

But it is not *just* the pubs or restaurants facing financial ruin that need my help. New businesses are bombarded with options and opportunities but lack the experience to know the right path to choose. Established businesses over time can lose clarity and direction. Using *The Five Star Formula*, I have been able to launch so many different hospitality venues that have hit the ground running from day one and are now established, thriving and award-winning five star businesses.

This book exists because I was struggling to work with everyone who was asking for my help. I am approached by endless business owners who have lost the love, energy and direction of their business. The pressure on them can quickly mount and they don't know which way to turn. With only twenty-four hours in a day, I needed a way to be able to reach more people and help them transform their businesses. I want to remove all the question marks they have about their venue and lay out the strategies I use to build and scale highly profitable businesses.

I believe this book is the answer.

The hospitality game is a tough one, but it can be made so much easier when you play with a better understanding of the rules. By going through this book and creating a plan for the improvement of your venue, you will, I hope, transform both your business and your life. The intended outcome of this book is that you will gain some knowledge and insight from my experiences and apply these strategies into the growth and success of your business.

*The Five Star Formula* has been used time and time again to both launch and transform hospitality venues of all sizes and empower them to be profitable, remarkable, and award-winning five star businesses. If you are willing to make some changes, keep reading and keep believing that the best is yet to come in your business.

*Joy Zarine*

SECTION ONE

# CLARITY

# CHAPTER 1

# WHY HAVE A FIVE STAR BUSINESS ANYWAY?

*'If you are not willing to risk the unusual, you will have to settle for the ordinary.'*

JIM ROHN

I can think of a number of businesses who manage to get it right, each and every time I visit them. Cocktail bars, restaurants, hotels, even coffee shops. They know what they are doing and have their performance levels and systems set so high, day in and day out, they rate as an undeniable five star business.

The reality is that every hospitality business can feel, perform and shine like a five star business. You don't need butlers, red carpets or silver service. You *can* have these things, but you definitely don't *need* them. What you need is a thriving business with passionate staff who create happy guests every minute of every day. Those guests in turn give you rave reviews, both online and in person.

But it's more than just having a guest leave happy – hopefully your business does that regularly anyway. What does having a five star business really mean and what does it feel like to own one?

Well, it means your reservations diary is fully booked throughout the year. Or perhaps you have people lined up to get in the door, every day of the week. You never feel concerned about whether people will visit your business. It is more likely you will be concentrating on how you can maximise the covers without affecting the service! You have waiting lists for the events you host with tickets being sold out the day you release them. You have a reputation for being busy, and people don't question why. They know exactly why – because yours is the best place around that does what you do.

Guests who visit your business feel delighted, excited and loyal to you and your vision. Even if something goes wrong, they know that is not the norm and they appreciate how efficiently the mistake is corrected. When an email hits your inbox announcing a review, you are proud, not fearful. There is no reason to feel fear – five star reviews are the absolute norm in your day. But they still make you smile because you can remember what it was like once upon a time when a review created a feeling of dread in the pit of your stomach.

You have a dedicated and passionate workforce. Your employees feel valued and excited about being part of your team. They tell their friends and family how much they enjoy working in your business and are always bringing in CVs of people they know who want to apply to join your team. You never have to advertise in the window or online for new staff – your office desk is packed with the details of prospective team mates.

You don't feel concerned whether workers will show up or do their job well. They are well trained and experienced enough to know they're working in a great business. They enjoy coming to work, and when they decide to move on to pastures new, they work their notice period and leave with great references and on great terms. They know they may want to come back to work with you again someday.

You don't have to spend hours and hours stressing over how to market your business to the public. You use Google ads and Facebook ads to improve your brand message to your ideal customer rather than a costly scattergun expense, week in and week out. Your energy is simply spent impressing the guests who walk into your business.

Newspapers editors regularly feature your business for free and journalists write articles about your events and new menu launches – for free. Your business picks up awards for customer service, community work or perhaps trend-setting in the industry. This collection of awards and commendations is admired by your guests and installs a sense of importance across the venue. Your competitors look to follow your every move, but you're not concerned with what they're doing. You have a specific vision and action plan for your business that will stand up to any political, economic or social changes.

Your reputation is rock solid and your business is here to stay. You never have to stress over the finances – you have money in the bank. Suppliers want to keep you happy rather than the other way around. Credit terms are relaxed; lenders know you're good for the money. Your bank managers, accountants and investors are all happy to see you because they are pleased with the numbers. Tax bills come and go, but there is plenty of money and cash flow to keep even the tax man happy.

And what about you as the owner of the business? You are able to sleep at night, knowing your time has been spent working *on* your business, not *in* it. You have a team around you who are hungry to learn from you and can cope with challenges when you are not there. You are able to go on holiday with family or friends, without fearing that the business won't be there when you return.

You have a clear plan for your progress, and for the important people around you. You are a fun person to be with, both in work and out of work, never feeling stressed, never having to shout. People actually enjoy spending time with you, and more than that, they value your opinion. You are respected as an industry professional – one of the good ones, who is successful and passionate, knowledgeable and friendly. Your approval matters to those around you.

Owning a five star business does all this. I know because I work with the creators of five star businesses, from independent restaurants to international brands. I see it every day.

The size or turnover of a business doesn't make it five star. It is far more complicated than that – it is the sections of the business, the causes, the effects, the repercussions, the impact and the memories that these places create. The owners are as relaxed as I have described, but they haven't always been.

I know what has made their businesses transform and I will be telling all to you in this book.

So why have you picked up this book? What are you looking to achieve?

I hope you would like to sprinkle a bit of five star magic on your business. Having a five star business that everyone loves is certainly not impossible, and I will guide you through the process of making this a reality not for a few weeks or months, but for the rest of your time in this business, and beyond.

Five star businesses are simply successful. They don't need to discount what they sell, come up with gimmicks and constantly reinvent themselves with new names, new logos, new websites. People know who they are, and rather than just liking what they do, they *love* what they do, and love *why* they do it. And these people tell everyone they know that they love it. Your competitors can't quite work out what is so special about you. But that's their business; it's nothing to do with you!

The reality is that customer service isn't just about someone opening the door for you, or pouring wine in a certain way. If it was, this book would simply be a long list of bullet points on how to serve a guest efficiently and with a smile. In the 1970s, that may have been all you needed. But in the 70's, when you had a gripe or a complaint about a business, you had to write it and send it into the business. The very person you were complaining about may have been the person opening the letter.

Nowadays people can write a review with the tap of a keyboard that will probably exist far longer than any of us will be on the planet. What a thought! Whenever someone wants to research your business, your reviews will be there. Forever. Some booking apps even list the most recent reviews next to the 'Book Now' button. A handful of bad reviews could result in your business missing out on hundreds or thousands of pounds worth of business.

Now, you can do what some business owners do and ignore the entire situation – think of everyone who has given you a good review as a genius and everyone who has written a negative review as spiteful or a village idiot. Or you can wise up and go after being better. Not just better, but the best. Top of the review pops; award-winning; the best in the business.

Sound good? Then read on.

# CHAPTER 2

# WHAT IS YOUR 'WHY'?

> *'The best advice I can give anyone is to spend your time working on whatever you are passionate about in life.'*
>
> RICHARD BRANSON

Before you make any changes or improvements to yourself or your business, I would like you to take a moment and reflect on your story so far.

Today we live in a world where something is always tugging at our attention. If it is not a telephone call or text message, then it is an email or Facebook or Twitter notification. We are constantly in demand, or at least it feels that way.

With so many distractions, it can be difficult to focus on what important things are happening in your life and in your business. It is not easy to concentrate on your role, your motivation and your purpose within your business when you're dealing with the urgent ring of a telephone.

All business owners know *what* their businesses do, some know *how* they do it, but not enough seem to know *why*.

Try and think about why you do what you do.

Why is it important to understand what motivates us? Well for one, when we know why we're doing something, we can be really clear about telling other people our motivations. When people understand why we are doing what we are doing, they can connect with us more and even believe in us more because of it.

Let me give you an example of what I mean.

Imagine a member of your family needs surgery. You go to meet two specialist surgeons to choose who will operate on your loved one. The first is extremely qualified. He has specialised in this area for over fifteen years and has won awards for his work. When you ask him why he went into surgery, he tells you, 'I am dedicated to helping people improve their lives. I remember my mother becoming very ill when I was a child and no one was able to cure her. I never want that to happen to someone else. So I went into surgery and I work every day with a passion for fixing people and changing their lives. Everyone I operate on I consider my life's work.'

In the office next door is another surgeon. He qualified at the same time as the first and also has many awards and commendations hanging on his office wall. When you ask the same question, though, he tells you that when he was studying at university as a struggling med student, he was in a lot of debt. He was told that surgeons earned more money than GPs so he decided to become a surgeon.

So which surgeon would you trust more? Who would you want to operate on your loved one? Both are as qualified as each other, but I would trust the first one every single time. It has nothing to do with the output of his work, but instead the reasons behind *why* he does it.

Now that's a pretty extreme example, but I hope it conveys the message of what I am getting at. When you peel back the onion and work out why you do what you do, it can have staggering effects on your business. Sometimes our motivation is the only clear difference between us and everyone else. This means it *really* matters.

Often when we look at brands or businesses we love it is not because of what they do, but why they do it. TOMS shoes are sold globally and loved by millions. They are stylish and comfortable, but in all honesty not much more than the next canvas pump. But TOMS have created an impact with their message of giving back. For every pair of TOMS shoes that is sold, a pair is donated to a person in need. Suddenly when we understand their motivation to make a positive change to the lives of others, buying a pair of canvas shoes has never felt so good.

For many people, hospitality was never in their plans from school. Doctor, policeman, solicitor and teacher seemed to be the only careers spoken about – the words *maître d'*, cocktail bartender or restaurateur were never mentioned. But when they tried hospitality, they were not only good at it, they really enjoyed it. This is certainly how I came to be working in this industry.

When I was eighteen and not sure what I wanted to do with my life, I started my first full-time job in a restaurant. I was passionate about the drinks I made and the food I served. I was able to go to work every day and really enjoy my role of making people happy, working with people I liked, which in turn made me happy. We were having a positive impact on people's days and it felt good.

So what was my 'why'? Why did I do that job? Ultimately, I thrived on being able to make people happy, and I still do. Having a guest trust me with their most precious asset – their time – and their second most precious asset – their money – feels like an honour. When I see guests in one of my venues, I want them to leave with great memories of their time there, knowing we are the best at what we do. Their satisfaction is everything to me.

So what about you? What are the 'whys' of you as an individual:

- ★ What motivates you?
- ★ What is your passion?
- ★ What is the mission of your business?
- ★ Why do you do what you do?

For example, your 'whys' might be:

- ★ To bring diverse food to suburban towns to celebrate and connect two cultures.
- ★ To create an elegant but accessible eatery that brings families together.
- ★ To combine contemporary, quality cocktails with classic food with integrity for guilt-free luxury.

Why is it important that I ask these questions? The answers you have written down affect not just your future, but the future of everyone who comes into contact with your business. The employees, the guests, the suppliers – everyone. Because if you can work out what drives you and makes you a part of the business, incredible things can happen.

In the famous Ted Talk 'Start with Why', Simon Sinek demonstrates the importance of this point beautifully. (You can watch it on YouTube – a great twenty minutes of exploring this idea.) He tells us that people don't buy *what* we do, they buy *why* we do it.

If you can find and articulate your why, your team, your guests and even your critics will understand what your business is really about. Being crystal clear about the why forms a connection with your team on a genuine human level. Convey it in a simple message and you may even change what your business stands for. The why ultimately affects the how of what you do, and understanding the why can lead to the creation of the core values or purpose of your business.

So it all starts with you asking, 'Why?'

# CHAPTER 3

# UNDERSTANDING YOUR BUSINESS BETTER

> *'People buy what they want,*
> *not what they need.'*
>
> DANIEL PRIESTLEY

Too often I see business owners' and managers' time being spent dealing with low level tasks – chasing suppliers, filling gaps in rotas, and ultimately rushing around to try and keep things moving. This is obviously not a productive use of their time, but it also prevents them from getting their heads out of the daily grind to see the big picture.

It is essential to make room to work *on* your business rather than simply being *in* your business.

Before you look at improving your business and taking it to a level you may have only dreamed of, it is important to understand the dynamic of the business you currently have. What are the major strengths of your business? What are the weaknesses? One of my most important jobs when I start to work with clients is to hold up a mirror (metaphorically speaking) and show them what their guest experience is *really* like.

It is important to understand:

★ What do people love about your business?

★ What do they hate about your business?

It can be an uncomfortable feeling when someone criticises our business. Our businesses are our creations; the manifestation of our passions; our babies. It is natural to want to defend and protect them at all costs. I feel that way about my businesses.

But the reality is, if we don't know what isn't working well, what isn't connecting with our guests and what is letting all our good work down, it is pretty much impossible to fix it. Your business is not perfect – no one's business is. We all need tweaks and improvements. Even the Ritz and the Savoy get negative feedback once in a while.

Understanding your guest experience puts you in a huge position of strength. Too many businesses focus their time, energy and money on attracting new people, when if they fixed their shortcomings, their audience would never leave. It's like pouring more and more water into a bucket that is riddled with holes. Working on your business like a pro rather than like an amateur is what sets it apart as a five star business.

For example, in the world of motor vehicles, amateur drivers bundle along on their journey, ignoring the warning signs on the dashboard, only stopping to pump up a tyre or fill up the tank when it is absolutely necessary. The professional F1 drivers, on the other hand, surround themselves with a team of people who know their role and work on doing it quicker and better every single time. The professional driver and their team fine-tune the engine, obsessing over improvements, practising and tweaking with every single lap.

What would happen if you approached your business in the same way, fine-tuning and improving it with every single guest?

Only when you understand the truth about your business, the guest experience you want, can your team deliver that vision for you. Once you know what you want to provide, you can do a better job of marketing that to your guests and potential guests. Remember – people buy what they *want,* not what they *need.*

When someone buys a hammer and a nail, what do they want? A hammer and a nail or a hole in the wall? Though these two answers are technically correct, another is the actual truth. No one wants to own a nail or a hammer, or a hole in the wall. What they want is to hang their picture and enjoy looking at it and having it admired by their friends and family.

So what is the ultimate truth in your business? Do your guests come because they are thirsty or hungry? Is it because they like the taste of Jack Daniels or want to eat a bowl of pasta? These may be true, but it's more likely they want something else entirely. What is it that *connects* people to your business? What does your business offer? A feeling of luxury? Community? Individuality? Health and well-being? Friendship? Romance? Excitement? Celebration? Fun? Are you an indulgence for once a year or an everyday part of someone's life?

You need to know this, and it's not always easy to understand as there may be a crossover in the experience you provide. A restaurant may accommodate a couple for a date night and a large group celebrating an important birthday celebration. You need to understand what you are to people and what they want from your business. Beware of trying to be something to everyone – you run the risk of pleasing nobody.

When you work on building a business that is guest-obsessed, the answers become far clearer. An awkward guest (I'm sure you can picture one right now – we all have them) may not appear to get what your business is. They want your cocktails to be bigger, your meals to be cheaper, the music to be quieter and the experience to be completely different from what it is. That person is *not* your perfect customer – and you, of course, can't please everyone. But when you know who you are aiming your business at, what that perfect customer really wants from you, you are able to connect your business with a future that may never have been possible before.

Peeling back the layers of your business and understanding the story so far sets you up to shape the future. Once you understand exactly what has happened, you can hopefully identify several aspects that you are proud of and that are working well, and several aspects that need attention, training and/or improvement.

Every business can have shortcomings in their offering or experience. Our guests may forgive and forget these things in the short-term, but if they never get looked at or improved, guests may end up going elsewhere. And who can blame them? People generally want to support their local high streets, independent restaurants and cafés, but as consumers they can't overlook poor service or poor experience forever. A new business may get a few months' grace for teething problems, but pretty soon consumers want to be wowed and proud of where they spend their precious time. As businesses, we must give our guests what they want, better than anyone else, every time. Life is too short for bad experiences.

I have worked with so many business owners who tell me there is nothing more they can do to improve. 'We've tried everything. We know we're the best we can possibly be.' And it may *feel* that way. Or sometimes people fall into the trap of spending their time and energy finding excuses for the failings within their business. There's no point in saying that if only your pub garden was sunnier or your licence was later, you would be more successful. Anything that *can't* be changed – well – can't be changed, so put your effort into changing what you can. (This may require thinking outside of the proverbial box.)

I remember working with a pub landlord who told me that his business would never be successful until he was able to have a bigger carpark. People needed to drive to the pub and park, and as long as they couldn't, he would be trying to service an empty pub. Now the food was great in this pub, the drinks were reasonably priced, so it did seem he had a point. But no one was about to knock down their house or give up their back garden to make way for his pub carpark.

After a quick session of calling local cab companies and asking if they would be interested in partnering with the pub, the landlord and I arranged three meetings. Three rounds of coffee later, we made a deal with the biggest cab company in the area. Its drivers would actively promote taking people to the pub, especially guests from the local hotels and B and Bs who were not familiar with the area. The pub landlord installed a direct dial telephone in the foyer and was assured the cab firm would give him priority status, especially at closing up time.

We then launched an advertising campaign, encouraging guests to leave the car at home to enjoy the pub's array of wines, ales and spirits. Takings over the next year went through the roof. So the bigger carpark wasn't the *only* solution to the problem. There is, as the saying goes, more than one way to skin a cat. Sometimes you need to explore alternative options to solve the main problem.

Basking in our triumphs and victories, breaking sales records and selling out events feels amazing. But when you are able to shut down the negative reviews by fixing something that has been holding you and your business back, that feels pretty incredible too. Trust me!

Confronting the truth about our businesses puts us head and shoulders above our competition. Understanding the numbers (sales, margins, spend per head, etc.) is one thing, but measuring the experience and identifying the shortcomings can be just as powerful. This requires honesty, but look at it not as a quest to find your failings, but as a fact finding mission to improve your business.

What in your business are you incredibly proud of? What five items would you hang in your hall of fame?

What are you embarrassed about in your business? What five items would you hang in your hall of shame?

Rating your business against itself is powerful. By tracking your feedback and other measurables in your business, you can make sure you are always hitting the 1% better than yesterday mark. Because that's really all it takes.

Imagine if you and your team went out to be 1% better every time you unlocked the door. Imagine what your business would look like 365 days from now. There's a lot of improvement to be made by very small changes – raising the bar of performance ever so slightly, every single time.

# CHAPTER 4

# YOUR MISSION AND YOUR VISION

> *'If you don't know where you're going, any road will take you there.'*
>
> UGANDAN PROVERB

The choices available for today's consumer are endless. Beyond endless. You can buy a burger for home cooking from the supermarket for 50p, have one made for you at McDonald's for 89p, head to Five Guys for a £10 burger, or Burger & Lobster for a £20 burger. You could even order a barbecue, coal, matches and beef patties from Amazon for delivery within an hour, though the weather staying good in the UK may be a little less reliable.

But the noise surrounding these choices is relentless. Finding a mission and vision behind what you do enables you to stand out to the world with a different message. One that isn't trying to sell anything, but is merely informing people.

The audience of this message can then make a decision. Do they connect and identify with that message? Do they agree with it? Can they believe in its authenticity?

Mexican grill restaurant Chipotle is a great example of this. Its mission is to help make the world a better place through food, transforming the industry and showing that it is possible to serve 'Fast food with integrity'. Chipotle believes in ethical farming of food with high-quality ingredients. On its website it states, 'With every burrito we roll, or bowl we fill, we're working to cultivate a better world'.

Now owning a restaurant that gives a fair price to the farmers without intensive farming methods, ensures livestock have a happy life, and pays the servers a respectful wage on top comes at a price. Ultimately the chicken costs more. A lot more. But people are happy to pay because they believe in the why. They want to live in a better world with good food in it.

Chipotle's adverts are famous for not even mentioning or displaying a single item that it sells. They are all about its vision of creating a world with environment and food ethics at the forefront. There are millions of people who agree with these ideals, and Chipotle knows its market and sells to it.

Now if consumers don't care about happy farmers, or happy chickens – that's OK. Perhaps they're more price conscious, but they understand Chipotle's mission and sidestep its restaurants to head to KFC. Chipotle wasn't built for everyone who loves to eat chicken; it was built for those who want to eat responsibly-farmed chickens that have had a happy life. Big difference.

## Finding your mission

Your mission statement defines the purpose of your business and what your business will do to make your guests' and/or employees' lives better. You need to articulate what your business does, and define yourselves against everyone else in a similar sector. What makes *you* special?

Finding your message or mission and sharing it with the world, you give people information and a better opportunity to choose you. Your mission describes your company's essence, helps employees stay on target and lets guests know what to expect. The people who fall in love with your message can visit your business with confidence, knowing it appeals to them – and then fall in love with what you do. Those who have no connection with what you do and why you do it can go elsewhere and take their negative reviews with them. After all, you can't mean something to everyone, but you can be everything to someone. Making that change can clear up a lot of stress and ill feeling from the day-to-day running of your business.

Hopefully your mission will be smart, simple and achievable. It is the purpose of the business, the reason for its existence. It should outline what is attainable over the next couple of years.

★ What do you do?

★ Who do you do it for?

★ What is your purpose?

## Finding your vision

Your vision statement describes what your business will be like in the future (maybe ten+ years from now). If the mission is successful over time, you will arrive at your vision. A vision statement is inspirational. It requires you to have big dreams.

Use the words to paint a future that is clear and easy to understand for anyone and everyone. Your vision may be to be a multi-award-winning restaurant, or to have 100 sites across the country. Perhaps your vision is to productise your business and sell your own sauces or cook books. Your vision should be personal, aspirational but adaptable.

★ What do you want to achieve?

★ How will your business grow?

★ How will you measure that your business is a success?

Your vision statement is a map to help everyone understand the journey your business is on, from the team working on the floor to your guests, your suppliers, your bank manager. Even your family members may struggle to understand why you're doing what you do. Understanding what your business is setting out to achieve is vital for everyone, leading to more engaged teams and guests. These few words could not only change your business, but ultimately your life and the lives of those you care about.

Revisit your mission and vision regularly. The more successful your business becomes, the more people will want to put shiny, bright opportunities in front of you. When these come up, be sure to ask yourself whether they align with your mission and bring the business closer to your vision. The answer will help your decision making.

What does success mean to you for your business? You can't get to where you want to get to if you don't know where that is. What is the mission for your business over the next twelve months? What is the vision for your business over the next ten years?

Creating a clear vision for your business is not the only action I would advise. Your life is, of course, more important than your business and needs proper consideration in creating a vision as well. What are *your* long-term plans? How do *you* see your life panning out both in the business and outside of it? I often find that successful people are active in directing and manoeuvring their lives, whereas many others can end up allowing circumstances to govern their future.

Having a vision for your life can keep you on track to achieve great things for you, your future and those you care about. Living intentionally rather than by accident is the only way to guarantee a chance at greatness.

Ask yourself:

- ★ What do you want your life to look like?
- ★ What do you want a day in your life to look like?
- ★ What is important for you to achieve and by what age or milestone?

Many of us can look back at a period of our lives when we didn't really have a plan and would just deal with life as it came up. For some it was when they were at school or university, perhaps their entire twenties. Some may never have had a plan.

For me, I would not have achieved much if I had not had a plan for how I wanted my life and my business to grow and evolve. With many clients, when I understand what it is they really want long-term, I can help make their dreams a reality – or at least bring them a lot closer to achieving them.

One of my clients told me when we met that he wanted to create a restaurant that people got excited about going to. He wanted his restaurant to serve epic food, world class cocktails and be so good that it won awards. He also told me some big, scary personal goals. He made the vision for both his business and his life crystal clear, so we knew what needed to happen.

I'm pleased to say that within a month of opening, his restaurant was fully booked, and within a year it became multi-award-winning. His mission for his business now and his vision for the future helped make this a reality. We were able to draw a roadmap and achieve many great things one step at a time.

Keep focused on the future for both you and your business rather than the past. Prepare to dedicate time, energy and money to achieving your vision. The time for sitting back is over. It is time to start building the dream.

# CHAPTER 5

# BUILDING YOUR DREAM

> *'Don't let your learning lead to knowledge.*
> *Let your learning lead to action.'*
>
> JIM ROHN

Now you have a vision for the future of your business, you need a plan of how to achieve it. What foundations do you need in place to build a long-lasting five star business? Building the dream is a continuous process – a journey of analysis, systems, results and improvement.

Around your vision there are three areas you need to work on in your business: the culture, customer and creativity. We'll be exploring each of these throughout this book. They become the pillars of your business that the vision will be built on, step by step and day by day.

If you don't make firm plans, your days can run into weeks, your weeks into months, and then you're a year down the line still trying to make changes without knowing when or how. By focusing on each area and guiding you through transforming and improving your business, I hope to encourage you to take every opportunity to make your big dreams a reality.

Let's explore.

## Culture

A culture of commitment and loyalty within your workforce is essential to a five star business. Building your business can be overwhelming with all the tasks you have to tackle, but you cannot grow just by learning to do more or do everything. Instead, focus on being a better leader, able to guide and grow your employees from a workforce to a dedicated tribe.

I don't believe that learning to attract top managers to your business is the best solution for your problems. Headhunting the world's best restaurant managers may not be the sticking plaster (or Band Aid for my American friends) to fix your shortcomings. You don't need them, and the truth is you probably can't afford them.

The skill you need is to see the potential in those around you. Attract people who are not only inspired but committed to your vision. You can't teach passion; you can't teach someone to care. Instead, you need great people who understand your plan for the business, believe in it and are dedicated to creating it.

## Customer

Creating loyal guests in your business is like finding the goose that lays golden eggs. Loyal guests allow you to get to know them, and in turn they get to know your business. This two way relationship enables you to target your offering towards them and similar people.

When your guests love what you do over a long period of time, you bank good grace with them, which means they will forgive you with ease if something does go wrong. Perhaps more importantly, though, they not only support your business, they can't help but tell the world about how wonderful it is. A personal recommendation is worth its weight in gold.

Too often I speak to business owners and managers whose mindset and conversations concentrate on their competitors rather than their customers. From menus to decor, website to hearsay around guests' experience, they become obsessed to learn all they can about what the business down the road is doing and selling and saying. What a waste of time and energy!

We won't become the best at what we do by focusing on anyone except our customers and our potential customers. I often feel like we are getting lost in a world of talking about marketing, insights and reach, and it distracts us from the conversations we should be having with our guests.

In order to win with our customers and our potential customers, we need to focus on three things:

★ Who are the key guests for the business?

★ What do they expect from us?

★ What do we do that disappoints them?

When this and only this is the focus of conversations with guests, our vision becomes clear on what we need to do to improve and grow the business. When we stop ourselves looking on the other side of the fence, we can tend to our own garden.

## Creativity

Being creative within your business involves exploring the new, and the unknown. It is not about just coming up with great ideas, but trialling them, testing them, improving them and committing to being better. Stand out and be different to everyone else, because nowadays slow and steady does not always win the race.

Being creative with your business is not for the faint-hearted. It can often feel safer to follow someone else, allowing them to set the trend, lead the way, take the risk, and then simply fly behind them out of harm's way. But in today's times, more than ever, fortune favours the brave. Apple didn't become one of the world's leading innovators by following Nokia's or Blackberry's lead. Customers follow creativity – it is what will raise you above and beyond everyone else.

By separating these areas, understanding them better and creating a plan of how to improve them, you'll have a strategy to take your business to the next level and be on the way to five star status.

# CLARITY RECAP

★ Having a five star business enables you to create better experiences, build a greater reputation and ultimately make more money doing what you do best

★ By knowing your purpose, you inspire not just yourself to be better, but those around you to support your business

★ Peeling back the layers of your business and really understanding the story so far sets you up to shape the future

★ Finding your mission and sharing it with the world gives people information and a choice, so you connect with people who not only love what you do, but also why you do it

★ Building a five star business is a continuous process – a journey of analysis, systems, results and improvement.

PURPOSE (+) VISION (+) MISSION (=) CLARITY

**Take Action:** Download the CLARITY Workbook via www.joyzarine.com/formula

SECTION TWO

# CULTURE

# CHAPTER 6

# HOW TO CATCH BUTTERFLIES

> *'Customers will never love a company until the employees love it first.'*
>
> SIMON SINEK

One of the biggest challenges faced by business owners in all industries is how to create a positive culture within the workforce. For global powerhouse brands to small independents, igniting a burning passion in an employee and getting them to care beyond the next paycheque can be difficult. Hospitality is no different.

This is not just a matter of training and development, but creating a shift in employees' mindset, inspiring an attitude of exceptional service for the guests and loyalty and dedication to the business. For a team of three to three thousand, a culture can transform their performance, and it all starts with understanding their motivation – what is *their* why?

Just like in the second chapter when we held a magnifying glass over your motivations and aspirations for the future, to understand the team you have around you, you must understand what inspires them. What are their hopes for the future, their passions? Tuning in to what gets your people alert and excited could majorly impact your business for the better. Now if you are CEO of a chain of international hotels with thousands of staff, this may seem a little too taxing. But your management team can be briefed, and in turn can speak to their teams.

Across any business, no matter the size, strive to understand the will of the people, and you may just learn something. For example, your business may over the past three years have relied entirely on a workforce of University students working part time. No one left, no one was fired, and everything was coming up daisies. But come graduation day, suddenly your workforce is no longer there. Your business will fall into a curve of non-experienced staff who will take six months to be as good as their predecessors, and another couple of years down the line the cycle may even repeat itself.

Now I am not saying don't employ part time students – far from it. But you need to have regular dialogue with your team or teams to be able to understand what motivates them. How can your business assist in their plans, and how can it benefit from those plans?

Very few businesses (if any) depend on just one skill set or type of person. We all have different skills and abilities, and the variety of people in a team can really be the making of a business. It is important to understand what may be missing in your team so you can attract the right people to fit into your business and thrive, or what skills may be needed to improve the people you already have.

So often we look at other people's jobs and lifestyles and think, *Thank goodness that's not me*. And most probably they look at ours and think the same! We are all built differently, so when it comes to creating an incredible machine of people in your business, understanding their motivations, strengths and weaknesses can result in a happier and far more productive workforce.

Meet Lauren, a nineteen-year-old student and waitress from London. She's studying performing arts at university and is passionate and energetic about almost everything in her life. She is committed to her studies, but loves to enjoy herself too. Friendly, fun and bubbly, she is great with all kinds of people.

Her long-term career goal is to be a famous actress in the West End, but while she is studying, she needs rent money and flexible hours. She visits home three or four times a year, but other than that she is available for all the hours she can get and is happy to be called in at the last minute to cover sickness.

The restaurant where she works allows her to keep her tips because she is exceptional at service and wants all her guests to leave having had a great time. She uses her time in the restaurant as a chance to play the role of the bubbly waitress, the floor is her stage and the guests her audience. It is the perfect place to learn her craft.

Meet Emma, thirty-four-year-old mum of two from Brighton. She works weekends and one week night to earn extra money for herself and her family. She has set shifts every week so she can arrange childcare, and she loves working. It gives her a chance to be herself for a few hours rather than simply being 'Mum'.

She loves that she works with people who have become friends and is a good listener and mentor to the younger team members. She guides them through busy shifts with ease because she knows looking after guests is far easier than looking after young children. The part-time role allows her to get out of the house, have a few laughs and earn enough money to cover her bills. Guests and team members love her and her caring ways.

Meet James, twenty-eight-year-old assistant manager from Harrow. James is committed to making a career for himself within the restaurant chain he works for. He works full-time, often putting in extra hours to get the job done. Wanting to soak up as much training and skill as he can, he has aspirations of becoming a general manager and even an area manager in the future. He would like to have the finer things in life: the car, the watch, the five star holidays.

James is a real go-getter when it comes to his job. He needs to be pushed and challenged within his role. If he isn't learning and growing, he feels like he is not reaching his full potential and may look elsewhere.

Finally, meet Eddie, thirty-four-year-old grill chef from Nottingham. He is the proverbial 'Steady Eddie' who wants forty hours a week, no more and no less. He needs to be managed because at times he can fall into the lazy trap of doing the bare minimum. Not overly money motivated, he would prefer to have something of an easy life.

Eddie lives with his girlfriend and their young daughter and is not concerned with the drama or politics of the workplace. He wants to clock in and clock out, and will do not much else within work other than what is required of him. Happy to work within clear guidelines set out for him, he is not prepared or willing to deviate from those terms at any time.

Why am I telling you about these people? They are all real examples of people who have worked with me or my clients, and they are all unique in what they want and give back to the business. They all require different ways of getting the best out of them, and this is something you need to consider for every member of your team. What motivates them? What gets them excited? What would make them leave? What currently makes them stay?

The reality is, no matter how many different people you have in your team, probably none of them will ever care about the business as much as you do. And nor should they. They haven't taken the risks, and they most likely won't be the person there to reap the rewards. It is not their baby – it is yours. However, by understanding the *why* of those around you and connecting to the journey of their dreams, you'll end up with a far stronger business. Create a synergy between your goals and their goals and make everyone a winner.

## Grow a garden

So how do you catch butterflies? Buy a huge net? No, you grow a beautiful garden. An attractive option matters to your potential workforce. Be aware of that and make your business a great place to work, and you can attract great people. Ensure your teams are involved in plans for the growth of the business and their futures. But be realistic about the length of service you can expect from some of your team. I assure you, a great employee for six months is better than an average one for three years. (Repeat this a thousand times a day until you believe it.)

Concert and events venue the O2 uses beautiful and talented 'resting' actors as a concierge service. London is an expensive city to live in, and aspiring actors need regular work that is flexible. Everyone gets trained in the job. If an audition comes up, someone else steps in to cover the shift. Shifts are limited so there is always a desire for people to want more. The O2 now has hundreds of bright-eyed starlets who are excited to be looking after special guests and VIPs. Everyone wins, and the venue has become one of the UK'S most famous success stories.

Creating a synergy between the needs and wants of your business, you as a leader and your team will not happen by accident. You will need a structure that creates conversations and honesty with everyone so you can guide them and get the best out of them.

I think back to managers from early in my career who could have got so much more out of me if they had only asked what I really wanted. Have regular one-to-one conversations, asking your employees about their take on the changes and growth in the business. Make it a mission to come out of each conversation with a deeper understanding of the outcome they want for the next few months. This could change their role, their development plan and future. If you're able to make your business stronger by making your team better, why wouldn't you? Be clear about what motivates people, and how you can help them to feel connected with their dreams.

# CHAPTER 7

# LEADERSHIP IS A CONTACT SPORT

*'A leader is one who knows the way, goes the way, and shows the way.'*

JOHN C. MAXWELL

The terms 'leader' and 'manager' are often used interchangeably, but they mean two completely different things. Managers instruct people on how to do something, whereas leaders encourage people to do things better than anyone else. Managers make decisions for the short-term, but leaders plan and act for the long-term. Managers follow the rules, leaders make up their own.

It is often said people don't leave jobs, they leave managers, and this is certainly true within hospitality. Being an effective leader gives you the opportunity to inspire the team around you and educate them on how you want things to be done. Leadership enables you and your business to become investable – after all, managers are replaceable within a business. Successful leaders become people of status, influence and inspiration.

So, what does **LEADERSHIP** really mean?

**L – listen.** This can be a challenge for many people. Everyone has an opinion in hospitality – and many opinions are given without being requested.

Just listen and take everyone's opinion on board. You don't need to make any changes if you don't ultimately agree with them. Some ideas may be in direct conflict with the values and mission of the business. They are right for someone, but not for you.

Fresh eyes can, however, give you a brand new insight into your business that you may have never considered. New employees or seasoned guests all have perspectives that are worth taking a few minutes to understand.

Learn to listen effectively, and don't be afraid to…

**E – encourage.** Encouraging your team (and yourself) to be constantly striving for more is a huge part of leadership. Keep positivity and motivation at the heart of every contact you have with them. Team members always need to feel motivated to give their best work and that their contributions are valued.

During tough periods in the business or in someone's personal life, a great leader will be there to encourage the team, letting them know that they are still pushing forward to achieve great things together.

**A - authority.** Being everyone's friend may make people around you gush at the Christmas party, but a good leader makes the tough decisions that can sometimes prove unpopular with the team. It's important, though, that you do so with all the facts, understanding the bigger picture and not letting friendships or relationships skew your thinking. At times of crisis, keeping calm and instructing people in the right way can turn tragedy into triumph and a problem into a huge opportunity to shine.

It takes authority to lead the way.

**D - delegation.** Create a team of talent around you to help deliver the vision of your business. Being successful does not mean doing everything yourself – in fact, it's quite the opposite. Determine what tasks to delegate and oversee their progress every step of the way.

When you look at the big picture, map out the smaller steps that will help you achieve your business goals. Planning day-to-day delivery and matching projects to the aspirations of team members will make success that much more attainable and feel more satisfying for everyone involved.

**E - energy.** Keeping both your and your team's energy levels up can really drive home results. Though you don't have to be the life and soul of the party, being upbeat with positive energy will make the world of difference to those working around you. Surprise and delight your team to keep their smiles beaming – positive vibes are infectious. Also, noticing when someone around you needs to take a break for a day or two is just as important as noticing that in yourself.

**R – recognition.** This point is so important it deserves a spotlight shining on it. It is too easy to get busy and forget to say, 'Thank you'.

Knowing how and when to thank individuals or teams for a job well done is as important as knowing who to ask to complete a task. A heartfelt thank you goes a long way to motivate your employees and inspire those around them.

**S – study.** We are living in remarkable times where technology is changing how we do business, how we interact with one another, how we learn and even how we fall in love. Never stop learning – the world is constantly evolving, and you need to move with it. If your competition is learning and you're not, you'll be left behind.

Iconic fashion brand Chanel was left slightly red-faced when the Instagram account @Chanel was claimed in 2011 by a teenager named Chanel Bonin. Chanel's lawyers have been fighting to take over the address, but so far the young woman has been able to fend them off. It's her name and she claimed it first.

The point of the story is, of course, to be in touch with trends. Chanel missed out because it didn't see Instagram as a relevant medium for its audience. Wow, what an error in judgement!

Learning and staying on top of trends is not below any of us. From the product you sell to how you are marketing your events, to the platforms you are communicating on, twelve months is a very long time in business. Keep studying and bring other people along to grow too. Your business will thank you, and your competition will most certainly not.

**H – high standards.** Define what having high standards *really* means, and make sure everyone understands what they are and how to achieve them. What do your key guests expect from your business? Make sure your high standards are achievable each and every day. Be consistent with these standards, from the first person walking into the building to the final guests at the end of the day. If a cup of coffee costs the same at 9am as it does at 9pm, the experience had better be as good whenever a guest orders it.

**I – inspire.** Working hard is admirable, but be sure to work hard with a purpose to have a life you love, enjoy and are proud of. Inspire others to do the same, and to enjoy their successes and work through the challenges.

The best leaders make a lifetime's worth of impact on those around them, and there's no reason why one of those leaders can't be you. We're inspired by those who push the boundaries, have big wins and smile through the ups and downs of the process. The struggles have to be worthwhile, so be sure to treat yourself and live a happy life that motivates those around you.

**P – plan.** Never stop planning, and never settle for mediocrity. When you don't have a plan or a target to shoot for, it's like playing a game without rules. There's no triumph, no glory and nothing to celebrate.

Creating a plan for one week/three months/six months/twelve months will keep everyone's eyes on a prize. It doesn't need to be sales driven; it might be the number of five star reviews in a period, or the number of team members passing a certification challenge.

Make sure you plan what you want to achieve, how it can be achieved and how it will contribute to your long-term vision. Keep planning, keep dreaming, and you'll never look back again.

Ultimately this chapter is all about becoming a great leader and building up your tribe. If the people around you are questioning your direction, that's OK. You need to paint them a clearer picture of the future and make steps towards going there. If people can't buy into it, maybe it's not for them, and that's OK too. This is your business and you need to work hard with great people around you to make it a reality.

The secret to building the right culture within your business is to be the leader your team needs you to be. Turn them from a team into your tribe.

# CHAPTER 8

# WALKING
# THE TALK

> *'When you believe in something,
> the force of your convictions will spark
> other people's interest and motivate them
> to help you achieve your goals.'*
>
> RICHARD BRANSON

Becoming a leader in your business doesn't just mean signing off the holiday forms, paying the bills every month and doing the jobs no one else wants to do. In order to be the leader a five star business needs, you must demonstrate the importance of everything that affects the guest, guiding your team to be better. Show consideration bordering on obsession for the happiness and experience of the guest. After all, if you don't care, why should anyone else?

The vision for your business should inspire you as a person. It is, I think, the most important driver for making someone a successful leader – which is why we started with understanding your 'why' and creating a vision. There are going to be lots of things you will want to develop and change within your business, but you will want to approach changes with tact and patience – like a game of chess, you need to move just one piece at a time. Change too much too soon and you could end up with more problems than you started with.

Stepping up to become an incredible leader will mean changing how you have done things before. Some around you may not want to see these changes or be able to respect what is happening. But being the leader must be something that resonates with you and that you work hard to deliver, every hour of every day. There is nothing more powerful than people seeing the 'big boss' deliver the level of service that they have been teaching others to achieve. People will realise that you know the job as well as they do, understand the struggles and difficulties they face. Never lose that.

The kind of boss who strides in swinging the keys, preaching empty words then sipping red wine at the bar with their pals does nothing but create a feeling of detachment and disrespect from the entire team. And yet that happens many times in many venues – I hope not in yours.

The truth is, to lead your team effectively and make the right decisions, you have to live and breathe your business. If you separate yourself from the team, their triumphs and struggles, your view can become skewed and your opinions somewhat irrelevant. Now I am not suggesting you pull pints or wait tables at every turn; that wouldn't make you an effective leader either. But there must be regular dialogue between you and your tribe. Be well informed enough to spot problems and issues either before they happen or before they majorly disrupt the service.

Spend the time to work on yourself and develop those around you to be great leaders and flag bearers of the business. When you know how you want your guests to be treated, what experience your business should be delivering, your actions must match your words. I'll say that again for emphasis – your actions must match your words. Speaking disrespectfully or negatively about guests or team members only allows those opinions to spread and the behaviour to grow.

Set high standards for the team around you and work with them to deliver it consistently. There are many urban myths around billionaires being caught picking up litter in their business; there was one in the papers last week. These stories always seem to generate surprise and become headlines, but I can never see why. I suppose many people imagine that a billionaire would not see the importance of tying their own shoelaces, let alone clearing up someone else's rubbish.

The way I see it, it is probably that sort of passion and dedication to the business that got the billionaire to where they are, and it never stops being their job to care. It is everyone's job to pull together, and if you show your team that this is everyone's job, there's no confusion. If it matters to you, it has to matter to everyone else.

Your life as a leader shouldn't just surround work, though. Leaders in hospitality, either hotel managers or restaurateurs, are not well-known for having an envious work/life balance. Our work often becomes our life and our life becomes our role, but it is important to make time for other passions outside of work, from sport to music, travel to rest. You want to create a tribe of followers in your team who look up to the life you have and aspire to have something similar.

## Training

When you are training your team, work on teaching them not just how to do things, but how you think about situations. You want your team to be skilled at thinking 'your way' when you are not even in the building. Role play workshops are perfect for this, practising for worst case scenarios such as difficult guests, emergency situations and high pressure thinking.

Giving your team an insight into how you have dealt with tricky situations in the past creates opportunity for them to learn and be better at the job they do. There is no substitute for experience, but it certainly helps to be prepared for when things go wrong.

## The daily huddle

Another essential to great leadership is the daily huddle. Getting together with your team for ten to fifteen minutes a day can set them up to succeed during that shift. We often see sports teams get everyone together to generate a winning mindset and discuss strategy, the team's vision and goals, and acknowledge the achievements up to that moment. This ability to take just a minute or two from what they are doing can be invaluable – sometimes the difference between winning and losing.

In your business, an understanding of what needs to be pushed, what isn't in stock and what kind of guests you're expecting tonight is essential to enable your people to perform at their peak. Huddle without fail before every shift to discuss opportunities to be better, previous problems and how to deal with them if they happen again, and send the team out on a positive note. Your team needs to feel appreciated, listened to and motivated. Be sure your huddles do that.

## Quarterly one-to-ones

Meeting regularly with team members on a one-to-one level is essential to keep them on track for the big vision of the business. You can then have direct dialogue and answer any queries or concerns people may have.

Explain the structure of the meeting to each team member beforehand, giving them the chance to gather their thoughts and be prepared. They should not feel surprised, ambushed or overwhelmed. Let them know what questions you have to ask them and give them a chance to bring their own. Hold the conversations within a safe space, out of the earshot of anyone else. Put aside more than enough time for the discussion so you don't have to cut it short to go somewhere else or meet the next person.

A one-to-one is an opportunity to share your vision and any changes that will be happening in the next few months. It is a time to celebrate achievements and focus on goals for the future; help your team members to understand their contribution to the big picture strategy and goals; discuss what isn't working or clarify any confusion there may be over certain tasks. Give your tribe a voice. Let them feel listened to, inspired and motivated for the new challenges ahead.

# CHAPTER 9

# RECOGNITION

> 'People work for money but
> go the extra mile for recognition,
> praise and rewards.'
>
> DALE CARNEGIE

I truly believe the most important words in business, any business, are 'thank you'.

We often spend time, money and effort saying, 'Thank you,' to our guests, making them feel appreciated, yet we do not spend half as much time on the teams we work with. Appreciation is a basic need for us as humans, and lack of it is probably the main frustration of many employees I speak to. When you go above and beyond in your job but this is met with no reaction from those above you, it's not likely to motivate you to do the same next time – why bother?

When we are recognised for the great work we do, it confirms that our work and we as individuals are valued. Recognition based on a positive performance in a task raises satisfaction and productivity.

Recognition is essential to creating a five star business. Great work deserves recognition, recognition creates energy, and you need energy to do great work. Your team members need to feel respected and valued for the part they play in the success of your business. If a thriving business does not recognise its employees' hard work and success, resentment can be quick to step in and take over. People don't leave companies; they leave managers – often because they feel undervalued.

So how can you future-proof your business to hold on to the best people and build a culture of growth and recognition?

I remember one company I used to work with that made sure recognition and rewards were always high on the priority list. Team members felt like they were more than just staff – as clichéd as it sounds, the company felt like one big, happy family. The managers organised regular local get-togethers, and annual trips to theme parks and bowling alleys. They held bar competitions, annual award ceremonies – there always seemed to be new ideas on how to say, 'Thank you for all the hard work'.

As the businesses grew in size and success, though, the managers began to focus on other areas. The cars they drove got nicer, their bonuses bigger, and the team parties and days out swiftly faded away. Those staff who had felt loyal began to feel dejected. The business continued to be 'successful', but the staff were unhappy.

When a company loses a culture of recognition, it shows. I remember hearing about a staff member being sacked for short-changing the guests and I couldn't believe it – he had been one of the most passionate and dedicated people in the company. Recently I saw him and asked what had really gone on all those years back, and his reply astounded me so much, I had to log it in this book so I'd never forget it.

He said, 'I stopped feeling cared about, and so I stopped caring.'

So why did this happen? It was the age-old problem of the company putting profit before people. Ironically, the company's profits soon took a dip because the great, dedicated people weren't there any more. The buzz had disappeared and it was now just like any other bar job out there.

How can you ensure the buzz of working in your business is kept alive and the profits kept up? When you are planning the growth of your company, don't forget to factor in rewards for those involved in achieving the success. When recognition and thanks become part of your business's DNA, your staff have a feeling of positivity, growth and success. Great people will gravitate towards your business and support it.

Recognising individual, team and the entire company's successes is so important, but of course, people are far more likely to achieve your goals when they understand where the goalposts are.

## Individual goals

Setting individual goals can make achievements feel really personal. We're all built differently, so when a manager sets a contest for everyone to take part in, some feel motivated and others find it too challenging. By setting individual goals, you can really connect each staff member with what they want to achieve. Give them the tools and teaching they need and encourage them to get there.

For some, the perfect goal may be to hit a personal best on sales. For others, it may be to recommend a particular drink, increase the spend per head in their section, or pass a knowledge test. Whatever it is, set a goal that is going to *mean* something to each individual and support their needs.

## Team targets

**Performance indicator targets.** Why not incentivise your team with something other than paper money? Set a target for the number of five star reviews you want to achieve in a month and give them great tools to achieve these. Print some business cards that say something like: '*Thank you for visiting us. If you've had a great experience, we would love you to tell the world* (add the web address of a review platform, e.g. TripAdvisor). *If there is anything we can improve, we would love you to tell us.* (Include your email address.)' Be sure every guest who looks happy and content with their experience gets a card, and keep reminding your team to strive for five stars.

Alternatively, incentivise the team to raise the ranking of your business on TripAdvisor to #1 in your area. Everyone, from chefs to waitresses, bartenders to managers, can directly affect the result, so it is the perfect team target.

**Buddy-up incentives.** Teaming up an experienced member of staff with a newbie and setting them a joint challenge can be great for everyone. Achieving a goal will help the newbie learn from a master and build a culture of support within your business. Make sure the reward is something they both really want, and allow the more experienced team member to guide the newbie to success. What a great test for potential managers, too!

**WOW cheque – daily recognition.** Empower your tribe not only to receive praise from the top, but also to give praise to each other. WOW cheques are great for this.

Make a stack of blank WOW cheques accessible to all team members at all times, and at the end of the shift, if anyone wants to reward a colleague for something that made them say 'Wow', they can. Examples could be going above and beyond for a guest, helping a new person learn the ropes, or cleaning someone else's section because they were busy. Whatever the reason, if someone spots something that impressed them, they can write out a WOW cheque and feed back to the team at the end of the shift.

Too often great things happen within the business that go unnoticed by those at the very top. WOW cheques give everyone a chance to shine a light on each other. They also create a level of constant awareness from your team, encouraging them to scan for excellence and be excellent at all times. Even the most difficult of shifts can then leave the team feeling good about themselves.

Why not surprise and delight your team by selecting a WOW cheque recipient and donor to receive a prize? The chance of a voucher, a treat or a special gift makes each WOW cheque even more important to earn.

# CHAPTER 10

# SET FOR SUCCESS

> 'Everybody is a genius. But if you judge a
> fish by its ability to climb a tree, it will live
> its whole life believing that it is stupid.'
>
> ALBERT EINSTEIN

A five star business rarely happens by accident. It takes a lot of planning, effort, and an entire team of great people.

Everyone has strengths, and as a good leader, you must shine a light on these strengths and develop them with responsibility. By encouraging every one of your team, you will make them feel motivated, appreciated, and hopefully inspired to do great things. Personal goals *and* team targets mean everyone has a destination that may lead to a reward, even if other people aren't pulling their weight. Unite everyone with the goal of being a five star business and connect this goal with the vision they have for themselves.

Keep your team focused on being better every single time. Good is never good enough; have everyone striving to be better – serve better food, better drinks, give a better experience with a better delivery.

So how can you guide everyone into being better?

**Be knowledgeable.** Get to know the people around you. It is not always possible to know every single employee (especially once you scale to multiple sites), but make sure the people around you are actively fact finding about what skills your business has and what it needs in the team. A selection of great people can ensure you make it successfully through every shift of every day with everyone knowing what needs to be done.

**Be clear about the role.** The responsibility of becoming a five star business (and maintaining it) falls on each and every one of your tribe's shoulders. From answering the phone and taking bookings to washing windows, managing stock control, cleaning the kitchen or saying goodbye at the door, no one is more or less important than the others. To succeed, be aware of every area of your business. Understand who is taking ownership of that area and how they can be better at it.

This does not mean, however, that team members don't help each other out. There needs to be a culture of support and having one another's interests at heart. But without designated roles and responsibilities, there are plenty of places for people to hide. You and your business have no room for passengers. If team members are part of the journey, they need to help lead the way.

**Reiterate the goal.** Map out a path to success for every one of your team. Their individual goals should align not only with your company's vision, but *their* vision for themselves too. If a team member has a dream of growth and development, you can help nurture it and ultimately get the best out of that person.

Keep regular conversations going, invest in training for your team, and bear in mind that it is better to have a great employee for six months than an average one for three years. By drawing your team members a clear roadmap to success, you will show them what they need to do and feel passionate about, and how to be part of a team that achieves great things.

**Getting your aces in the right places.** Everyone has something to contribute – your skill as a leader is to work out exactly what that is. Once you know people's whys and their skill sets, let the best in your business shine. If you have a communicator, give them the rotas to manage. Got yourself an organised introvert? Stock control, either front of house or back of house, is ideal to manage them, measure their performance and build their confidence. For the techy geek, there's till system updates or booking system maintenance. For the keen photographer there's Instagram; for the budding journalist, how about a monthly press release?

There is an important place and opportunity for everyone in your team, guided by you. You cannot and should not do everything. Allow the great people around you to find their passion, and let it thrive within your business.

**Tools for the trade.** Once you have found great people and they're doing great things, is it time to hit the travel agents and book that long-awaited world tour? Well, not quite yet. You must be sure everyone has the tools to make success, for them and for you, a reality, whether those tools are enough fridges to hold stock, enough stock to make drinks or enough training manuals. They may simply need an allowance from you to spend on their area of the business, but your business growth will grind to a halt if your team haven't got what they need to do their jobs.

A huge part of building a culture within your business is to build trust. As well as the items your team members physically need in order to do their jobs, are they getting the support in training and knowledge that they need? Training beyond the basics of day-to-day service is not often a priority for businesses. It can feel like a wasted expense, especially if employees take the skills they learn and go on to other jobs making someone else money. Well, that may all be true, but for now they are working for you. If you want them to do great things, empower them with the skills and training to do so.

CFO: 'What happens if we train them and they leave?'
CEO: 'What happens if we don't and they stay?'

# CULTURE RECAP

★ Be an attractive option for employees and you will attract the best people for your business

★ Understanding individuals' motivations is essential for getting the best out of them

★ Successful leaders are people of status, influence and inspiration for those around them

★ To lead your team effectively and make the right decisions, you need to live and breathe your business

★ People need to feel recognised as both individuals and important members of your tribe when they have worked well, achieved goals or put in exceptional effort

★ Good is never good enough; have everyone striving to be better

---

**LEADERSHIP (+) INSPIRATION (+) RECOGNITION (+) TRAINING**

**(=) CULTURE**

---

**Take Action:** Download the 'CULTURE' Workbook via www.joyzarine.com/formula

SECTION THREE

# CUSTOMERS

# CHAPTER 11

# GREAT EXPECTATIONS

*'Every day we're saying, "How can we keep the customer happy? How can we get ahead in innovation by doing this?" Because if we don't, somebody else will.'*

BILL GATES

Once upon a time, our ancestors would have had to forage and fight for food, living under a cycle of famine and feast. Our grandparents and great grandparents had to deal with the Great Depression, world wars and the rationing that followed. Life was not always plentiful; options and opportunities were often scarce. Choices were available to the few rather than the many.

Nowadays, though, the world we live in is different, and really, we have never had it so good. Despite recessions and credit crunches within my lifetime, I cannot remember a day when supermarket shelves were empty or the money in my pocket became suddenly worthless. The family that we are born into no longer decides our future or the future of our children. Smartphones are media centres, and the opportunities to make our own way in the world are literally endless.

So what has this got to do with you and your business? Well, we need to understand the psychology of how good we have it today and what that means for the guests visiting our business.

From the clothes shops to the restaurants, the takeaways to the taxi rides, whatever we want, we can have. Though perhaps that should make people happy and content, the truth is, they are not. Many people feel like they work harder than other generations, longer hours for less quality of life, and their free time has got to be spent feeling rewarded, feeling pleasured. And they expect it all to be perfect. We live in times of great expectations.

So why are people complaining now more than ever? Well, it could be that they've forgotten just how lucky they are, but the truth probably lies a little deeper. It could be that they are so spoilt for choice that when something doesn't go exactly as it should, they feel frustrated that they chose one place instead of another. It could be that they believe the hype they read online and see on Instagram, and when the reality of the food comes without the automatic filter, they feel let down. Perhaps the pressure to live and breathe perfection has them wrapped up in expectations that are too high. It appears society in general wants more in less time and for a lot less cost than yesterday. This is seen across industries from fashion to supermarkets, banking to homebuilding.

In our industry, it takes everything we've got to satisfy these great expectations each and every time. And human nature is not about to change. I wish I could wave a magic wand and suddenly guests would stop complaining, stop writing bad reviews and telling their nearest and dearest how awful their day was due to the chicken being too dry or the ice in their wine glass too cold. I can't. And neither can you.

This part of the book is not about trying to alter the mindset and expectations guests have towards our businesses, making them care less or expect less. Instead, it is about understanding what they care about, and more importantly, how we can ensure our businesses deliver on our promises each and every time.

Creating experiences that not only satisfy but also surprise and delight your guests is a huge step towards becoming a five star business. But how can this happen in a consistent way without *you* having to greet every guest and handle every complaint? How do you take on these challenging times and not only do well, but *exceptionally* well?

Well, there are three key things you need to know to improve guest experiences within your business.

## Defining your 'perfect' guest

We can't be everything to everyone – and nor should we try. The way to become a five star business is to know exactly whom we are targeting and work hard to attract and satisfy those people in particular. Of course, there are anomalies who we will attract and hopefully delight, but we have to become obsessed with knowing who we are working so hard for.

There are usually around three key guest personas for your business whom you can identify and learn to attract. For a city centre coffee shop, the three may be:

Patrick – thirty-five-year-old businessman who purchases two espressos and an artisan sandwich every day. He keeps up to date with sports news and current affairs on Twitter and his local football team in the newspaper.

Jessica – twenty-eight-year-old mum of two who enjoys catching up with friends over a latte twice a week. She spends time in her day on Facebook and Netmums when she is not looking after her young family.

Lauren – nineteen-year-old student who visits her high street coffee shop daily during her lunch break with friends for hot chocolates in the winter and iced smoothies in the summer. She enjoys using Instagram and Snapchat to keep in touch with her closest friends.

When you can personalise and understand whom it is you are talking to, suddenly everything, from new menu items to refurbishment decor to where to spend marketing and advertising budgets, becomes *so* much easier. You are no longer simply pleasing yourself or your team; you are learning to please your perfect guests – the people you actually want to be attracting to your business. When you obsess over their likes, their dislikes, their pleasure and pain points, your business ramps itself up past most others.

Finding your key guest demographics can truly unlock your potential for growth by creating great experiences that connect with their DNA.

## Understanding guests' expectations

Perhaps your key guests expect for you to take their coat and hang it in a cloakroom. Perhaps they expect linen serviettes and tablecloths. Does your key guest expect huge portions overflowing from the plate, *Man Vs Food* style? Do they expect to feel comfortable dressed in casual jeans and a T-shirt when visiting your business, or would they rather be stepping out in their finest threads?

By studying each and every one of your key guests, you can get into their mindset and not only understand them, but understand what they need from you to meet their expectations. You can then work on managing and delivering on those expectations. Whatever you say you're going to do or be, you can and *must* do or be it every time, and do it better than anyone else. Unless you understand exactly what your ideal guest wants from you, though, you could go to a lot of effort, be inconsistent and generally just not hit the mark.

It is also essential to understand the customer journey of your business. This journey does not simply start at the front door; the first step could be a potential guest visiting your website or social media platforms, or phoning to make a reservation.

So what do those experiences feel like? Are your key guests happy with what they see, hear and feel? Walk in their shoes and understand every step. Is the website smart enough? Does the reservations page look good enough? Is the person on the end of the phone knowledgeable enough?

The journey of your guest should be filled with great experiences that feel effortless for both them and the server. Some of the greatest experiences I have had have not been overly obvious ones. It wasn't what a business did that made me think, *Wow, that was awesome*, it was how the *experience* made me *feel*.

## How to attract your perfect guests

Becoming an expert in who your key guests are, what they love (and what they don't), gives you the ultimate tools to attract them to your business. If your key guests are passionate about wine or desserts, about live music or reality TV stars, you know what it is they are looking for in you.

A local nightclub whose key guests are aged eighteen to twenty-two, studying or working while living at home with a disposable income, could offer sweet drinks like cocktails and rosé wine that appeal to young people. If the guests love watching reality shows like *X Factor, Big Brother* or *TOWIE,* every weekend the club could have live appearances from celebrity guests from these shows.

It is great business to connect your perfect guests with their passions. Serve your key guests with something that is remarkable. It may not be suitable for everyone, but you're not trying to please everyone. Being everything to someone wins in the end.

# CHAPTER 12

# DELIVERING THE DREAM

> *'Good service is good business.'*
>
> SIEBEL AD

## Service standards

Delivering on your promises and the dreams you have for your business, of course, does not happen by accident. A set of standards – the absolute basics of good service – that everyone knows, understands and believes in will make your team's service better (and probably their tips too). For example, 'Twelve Key Points of Service' or 'Ten Golden Service Rules' can meet the needs of the guest within your business, every step of their journey.

One standard set of 'Twelve Key Points of Service' for waiting staff in a casual dining restaurant might be:

★ Greet your guest(s) at the door and seat them with menus

★ Take a drink order

★ Deliver the drinks

★ Explain menu features or specials

★ Take food order

★ Deliver the food

★ Two-bite check and offer additional sauces/drinks

★ Clear the table and present dessert menus

★ Take dessert and coffee/tea order

★ Deliver desserts/hot drinks, etc.

★ Offer anything else or the bill

★ Thank your guests as or before they leave and wish them a fond farewell.

Your business will need its own set of standards to suit *your* style and the vision for the service it provides. Your standards must align with your key guest's needs, wants and expectations. To make sure they are actionable, they must be memorable to everyone – most of all you. You as the leader of the business will need to know them, live them, teach them and spot when something has been missed. They have to be easy to execute every single shift – no matter how quiet or busy – and must be possible no matter how many team members are working.

Your guest doesn't need to know anything about the set of standards. They are there to enjoy themselves, their food, their company. The service should feel effortless and your guests should feel attended to. It is not about your guest remembering what it is you do. Rest assured, they will remember how you made them feel.

## Consistency is king

I remember visiting a restaurant several years ago and everything was perfect. Better than perfect, it was exceptional. I was greeted at the door by the host with such genuine warmth, I instantly felt welcomed and at ease. They asked me where in the restaurant I would like to sit, so I opted for a window seat facing the bustling high street below.

'Great choice,' the host said. 'I'm a people watcher too.'

Asking for a wine recommendation with my meal, I was presented with two great options and welcomed to try both so I could be sure of what I was ordering. After my meal, my coffee was poured in front of me, served with complimentary chocolates, and I was left to sit and enjoy the moment until I requested the bill.

The experience was sublime. I felt looked after and that made a lasting impression on me. So much so that a few weeks later I arranged to meet a client there for lunch to go over plans for a new project.

However, the experience felt different this time. There was no warm welcome; we were left to stand for a few minutes at the door before the host appeared. She didn't ask where we wanted to sit, showing us instead to a table near the kitchen pass. When I asked for a wine recommendation, she said abruptly that the house wine was very good. Coffee was served without a chocolate, and with the bill even though we hadn't requested it. The food was just as tasty as the first time, but the experience was not as remarkable. In fact, it felt somewhat underwhelming.

Six months later, I was back in the town and wanted to try the restaurant again. This time, the host told me to seat myself wherever I liked. She brought out wine options on request and again the food was excellent, but she offered no coffee this time, and the bill was presented once the plates had been cleared.

In isolation, each experience would have been good, but they felt completely different and that frustrated me. I was so impressed the first time and then let down again and again because everything felt inconsistent. When it comes to great customer service, consistency is king. Your guests want to love what you do, and expect you to deliver on every occasion.

The Starbucks experience is an interesting one. I have stepped into Starbucks in London, Paris, New York, even Mumbai, and the queuing system is the same, the decor is the same, the way in which the servers write down my order, is the same. The coffee looks, smells and tastes the same across the globe, which is pretty incredible considering my earlier example of one restaurant in one location that can churn out a vastly different experience every time. Starbucks has such robust systems in place that it can consistently deliver the dream.

If guests know and love what they're going to get, they will come back again and again. Life is too short for bad experiences (and bad coffee, in my opinion).

So how do you manage to get your business to be consistent? Systems, systems, systems.

## Building systems

When I talk to some small business owners about building systems, I am met with the response, 'That's not really what we're interested in. We're too small for all the formalities.' If you're a one-man food truck business, maybe that response is OK. You know what you need to do each day, and you're ultimately the only one who needs to know. But what if you're ill or want to go on holiday? Wouldn't it be nice to have a system that meant you could hand the business over sometimes?

If you're anything bigger than a solopreneur, you definitely need systems in place. There is no doubt in my mind at all.

So, what systems does your business need?

★ Systems to train

★ Systems to measure

★ Systems to market your business

★ Systems to make improvements inevitable

When you're creating your business, the systems within it are the building blocks that make your dream a reality. They will align with your long-term vision, and can give you more time away from the business, more profit, more growth and a greater value on the business if you want to sell it.

CHAPTER 13

# THE EXTRA MILE

> *'It's never crowded along the extra mile.'*
>
> WAYNE W. DYER

The waiter asks, 'Is everything OK with your meal?'

'Yes, thank you,' the guest replies.

Sound familiar?

This exchange happens millions of times a day across thousands of businesses. The food is served, the drinks are shaken, the bill is paid, and everything *is* OK. But is 'OK' ever really good enough? Don't we need to make sure we're going the extra mile in our business?

Five star businesses are built on the extra mile – the road less travelled. It sets us apart from everyone else, makes us better, more memorable, easy to recommend.

But how often do we concentrate on getting ourselves, our team and our business to go the extra mile? It can often happen by accident – the right person does the right thing at the right time and the guest is left surprised, delighted and with a feeling of 'Wow'. But I don't want it to be an accident in your business, or to rest on just one exceptional member of staff. Too often in business I see a star player at service going above and beyond, delighting the guests while everyone else lingers in the shadows.

I remember in one of my first jobs at a bustling themed restaurant many years ago, one waiter was the absolute star of the show. Everyone loved him because he always went above and beyond. This guy *only* operated in the extra mile. The sodas he served were always huge (and rarely added to the bill), the desserts looked twice the size of those on the menu, he gave out balloons in abundance – animals, swords, party hats, and giant giraffes. Guests sitting in his section beamed from ear to ear as he wowed them with magic tricks and birthday songs, and all the other guests looked on, wishing they were there too. He was exceptional.

But having an exceptional experience like the one he provided was a lottery draw. The rest of us didn't leave drinks off the bill to satisfy our guests; we weren't allowed to. Desserts were made to specification because they had to be. When we had a spare moment, we were running food to tables or washing glassware – not doing another magic trick. He was allowed to do what he wanted because everyone was in awe of him, management included. He had the happiest guests, the busiest sections and the best tips – he was, after all, 'the best'.

But looking back, I realise he *wasn't* best for the business. When guests came back and ordered the same dessert as they'd had the last time, it just wasn't as good as it had been then – because it had been made and served by someone else.

Beware of exceeding in a way that doesn't build your business; you'll be taking one step forward and two steps back. Going the extra mile isn't about empowering one person. It can't be. You want your guests to fall in love with what your *whole business* delivers, rather than with what one person delivers. Then rather than telling their friends, 'Our waiter was brilliant', they'll say, 'You have to try that place, it is incredible.'

So how can you go the extra mile as a team, as a business, each and every time? You need a plan of execution. What do your key guests expect? What will make them say, 'Wow, that's brilliant, thank you'?

## Indulge the senses

By indulging the senses of your guests, you can wow them time and time again. Each guest is an individual, and when we acknowledge their wants and needs by giving them great options and experiences, they feel cared for and understood.

**Toilets.** Be meticulous with the cleanliness and products in both the women's and men's toilets. Luxury soap, hand lotion, air scent dispensers, toilet paper – go with quality every time. Five star businesses cannot and do not compromise in that department.

Be sure to have a daily check of everything in the toilets, including making sure that door locks work and coat hooks are all present and correct. The small details that many businesses don't notice can make a guest feel either cared for or not cared for.

**Tooth picks, towels and wipes.** Oh my! If you're serving anything greasy or messy, such as ribs or wings, make sure you provide the correct accompaniments so people do not need to ask for them or leave the table to get cleaned up. Dining out should not become an uncomfortable or embarrassing affair.

**Scent within the building.** If you have one or one hundred restaurants or bars, a scent that sets the mood can be a subtle addition to the atmosphere. Nowadays, without cigarette smoke covering every surface (fortunately), we can be left with the smell of grease, sauces, beers or even bleach (unfortunately). Pick a fragrance that suits your business, and a few atomisers will give each outlet a sense of familiarity.

**Wine tasting.** Give guests the opportunity to try a wine before they order, with an alternative on standby if they wish.

**Music to suit the mood.** This should go without saying, but I have to mention it. Music choices cannot be down to the daily whim of the bartender or waitress on duty. Keep your key guests in mind, along with the time and the day of the week. Keep tweaking, keep improving – it can set the entire mood of the building and improve the spend per head.

**Pillows, chairs, cushions.** Comfort is, of course, key. For hotels, have a range of pillows available. For restaurants or bars, having a low or high chair available to suit a guest's needs can hugely transform their experience. If someone is on crutches or walking with a stick, it is a great indicator they may need special attention. Be aware and know how to help solve any issues before they happen.

**Temperature change.** Air conditioning is one of my biggest frustrations in many venues, simply because the temperature is controlled by the staff who are rushing in and out of a hot kitchen or busy frothing milk in front of the steamy coffee machine. Please be aware of the temperature for the guests. Indicators are people keeping their coats on, folding their arms and shivering, or at the other extreme, stripping off and fanning themselves with menus. Look for the signs, adjust accordingly, and don't be afraid to ask the guests.

**Thank you letter.** If someone sends a letter of praise or criticism, be sure to write to them and thank them. A handwritten letter these days is a somewhat lost art, but it can be a powerful demonstration of just how important your business is to them that they took the time and effort to get in touch. If a guest has written to you directly, appreciate that. Thank them, thank them, thank them. The cost of a stamp may earn you a loyal guest for life.

## Know your onions

**Learn the history** of your company, your building and the local area. If there are interesting facts to know, be sure you and all your team know them. When a guest shows interest in the local area by asking a question, a confused look and a shrug just won't cut it.

**Get curious about the products you sell** – your guests will be. If there is something interesting to learn about them, learn it. Wine, whisky, chicken or beef – know your onions!

**Taxi numbers.** Ideally, you'll have a preferred taxi company that will either give your guests special rates or speedier pick-ups. Be sure to know the numbers off by heart so you're not hunting for the *Yellow Pages* or on Google while your guests are keen to leave.

**Drink recommendations.** Knowing your menu isn't enough. You need to know how to recommend items, especially cocktails where people may be intimidated by the unknown. Ask questions such as, 'What are your favourite spirits?'; 'Do you like sweet or sour? Refreshing or strong?' Being able to pair their answers with great recommendations really takes your guests' experience up a notch.

**Recommendations for things to do.** For out-of-towners or people new to the area, it's a great skill if you can recommend suitable things to do in the area. Having a list suitable for each demographic in your mind is also important. Recommending ice skating to an eighty-five-year old or bingo to a sixteen-year-old is just unhelpful.

**Frequently Asked Questions (FAQs).** Know the questions people keep asking – there are probably many more guests who want to know the answers. Add the FAQs to your website and keep reviewing them to make sure they include everything people need to know about your business. Be sure everyone on your team knows the answers, too.

**Allergy advice and solutions.** As five star hospitality businesses, we have a responsibility to all our guests – including those with allergy or dietary limitations. It is not good enough to advise people on what they can't have; we need to provide them with something exceptional that they can have.

If you feel like it will be a strain on your holding stock to have gluten free or vegan options always available, for example, why not request twenty-four hours' notice from guests with special dietary needs and have a plan in place of what you will provide? It will make a huge difference to guests who are limited in what they can eat.

## Surprise and delight

**Phone chargers.** Love them or hate them, our mobile phones are an essential part of our lives. Be sure to have a couple of working chargers (for use with the most popular phone sets) available for guests to use if required. Such a small gesture can make a big difference to someone's day.

**Picture takers.** When there's a group out celebrating, offer to take a picture with everyone in. Group pictures are never the same when someone has to step out to take them. Surprise and delight your guests with your recognition of the importance of their event.

Why not have a Polaroid camera available to take a photo to give to the birthday boy or girl? A tangible memory to take home and treasure is remarkable.

**Taxis.** Keeping your guests warm, dry and content on cold, blustery nights is a must. Make sure your preferred taxi company is aware when you have busier than usual nights so they can be well staffed to cope with the demand. Offer taxi arrangements for large parties when they book to assure them they can leave the car, enjoy themselves and still get home with ease.

**Special occasions.** Keep a drawer well stocked with greetings cards for all occasions, signed by the staff and ready to present to guests who are celebrating with you. It really adds a personal touch to the event and lifts you far above any restaurant or bar they have visited before.

**Umbrellas.** When the rain is coming down and your guests are dressed in their Sunday best, it is a huge wow if you can supply them with branded umbrellas. Be sure to offer guests the use of an umbrella and ask them to pop back with it next time they visit. You've either secured free advertising for the next few years across town or a return visit from guests who will be grateful that you care. Well worth the few pounds each umbrella will cost.

**Emergency everything.** From safety pins, hair bands, plasters to superglue. If the birthday girl's high heel breaks or hair band snaps, being on hand to fix it could potentially save the day. For fewer than twenty pounds, an emergency fixing kit for most things is, I think, is essential – I never leave the house without mine.

## Excel with technology

**Website.** Your website is the digital window to your world – never stop working to improve it. Keep your regular key guests in mind when you are adding content, but also consider people who may not have heard of you, or who may not even know the area you are in. Include parking advice, transport links and nearby landmarks on your frequently asked questions page.

When you're building or developing your website, don't settle for average but affordable. Work with professionals – if you think they're expensive, wait until you work with amateurs! Keep everything up to date, and you'll be reassuring people that you know how to look after your guests before they have even stepped inside your business.

**Bookings.** Have a strict system, and make sure everyone on the team who comes into contact with guests making bookings knows the system inside out. If a guests calls a restaurant only to be met with a lot of umms and ahhhs and confusion, it simply won't do.

Booking apps can be great at keeping the flow organised, but they do come at a cost. Your key guests may prefer to pick up the phone and speak to someone. Make sure your business is prepared to impress.

**Special occasion invitations.** Make a note next to the booking if a guest is celebrating a special occasion and be sure to impress them a year down the line when you invite them back to celebrate again.

Bear in mind that your exceptional will one day become the everyday. When you're a five star business, your competition will keep a pretty close eye on you, so you'll have to keep tweaking, keep improving and keep building.

Being the best at anything rarely happens by accident. Don't be afraid to step up and exceed expectations, but you want your standards to come from the business via the employees. They must be sustainable. Being remarkable will cost you some money, but rest assured, when it's done correctly, it will generate a reputation of excellence that will bring in far more. People won't be able to help but tell everyone just what a special time they had in your business. You'll be hijacking many a watercooler catch-up when colleagues ask the eternal question, 'Did you do anything nice at the weekend?'

As your guest experiences improve, the recommendations will increase and people will be visiting you with their own great expectations. You must be aware of this and be prepared to deliver every single time. When the experience is right, your guests become walking, talking billboards for your business, and all you need to do is keep the standards high.

# CHAPTER 14

# THE EVERLASTING REVIEW

> *'The trouble with most of us is that we'd rather be ruined by praise than saved by criticism.'*
>
> NORMAN VINCENT PEALE

Once upon a time, many years ago, a guest in a restaurant was served poorly by a waitress and did not leave happy. Nothing shocking or out of the ordinary. It happened then and it happens now in most cities and towns every day. Soup is served cold, Chardonnay is served warm, it's all served without a smile – you get the idea?

Let's call this particular guest 'Lady Flowerpot'. In disgust, she left without giving a service tip, got home and wrote a strongly-worded letter to 'whom it may concern'. Perhaps it did concern someone, such as an owner or manager, and they replied filled with regret and good wishes. Or perhaps the letter ended up in the bin and no more was said about it.

Complaints once upon a time were on a one-to-one basis via direct mail. No one else would ever have known about them. Of course, something disastrous would get tongues wagging, but a negative experience was pretty far from becoming public property.

And then the internet was born and the world shifted.

Now, the pipeline of communication between two people, the guest and the business owner, has burst. A guest can write a complaint and publish it online, and every single one of us has front row seats. Customer review sites like TripAdvisor have exploded in popularity over the past five years. The Lady Flowerpots of today not only have a voice, they have a megaphone and a platform to stand on, and hundreds of thousands are there to listen and learn.

So why has this happened?

Well, TripAdvisor's mission states that it allows customers to gain the real truth about what to expect in a hotel, café, pub or restaurant. For consumers and customers, TripAdvisor can feel like a fun pastime – a way to peruse their next holiday destination or perhaps pick out a pudding recommendation for their next evening out. But for hospitality business owners, an email stating 'A review has been submitted to your profile' can drive fear and panic into the hearts of even the loudest and proudest.

It's not just TripAdvisor, of course. Other sites include Google Reviews, Facebook, Yelp, Zomato and booking apps such as OpenTable. Different review sites will come and go, but what is here to stay is the appetite people have to read and write reviews. The Pandora's Box of reviews has been opened and may never be closed again.

So who is writing these reviews? Statistics suggest it is mainly females between the ages of thirty and fifty-five, but the more important question to ask is *why* are they writing them?

**To be supportive.** Probably the most altruistic of reasons people write reviews is to be supportive of their fellow consumer and help them make an informed decision, be the review negative or positive. If a guest has had a great experience, they will want to let others know about it so everyone can have the same enjoyable experience as well. Despite how it can sometimes feel, most reviews submitted across sites are positive and complimentary about a business.

And if the experience wasn't so good, the review is an opportunity to warn others.

**To say thank you.** When a service, product or experience has been well received, people will want to say thank you in the form of an online review. The old saying goes, 'One good turn deserves another', and users of review sites can feel passionate about rewarding a business for a wonderful time with a great review.

**To give an 'expert' opinion.** Today we can all be food critics. And hotel inspectors. And experts in the art of hospitality. Because we have been given the platform to air our opinions, and humans feel their opinions are important. With little or no training, experience or understanding, we can tell the world whether something is wonderful or terrible just by how we felt about it.

**To feel listened to.** If your guest's experience was not perfect and there was no opportunity for them to give feedback, a review may be on the way. Or if an incident happened and the resolution was not satisfactory to the guest, they may well vent their frustration at the situation via a review.

This is how the guest complains now – for all the world to see. The public are reading the reviews, watching your responses and learning all the time about your business. So what can you do about it?

# CHAPTER 15

# WINNING WITH REVIEWS

> *'Don't let people's compliments get to your head, and don't let their criticisms go to your heart.'*
>
> LYSA TERKEURST

Dealing with negative reviews can feel soul-destroying. You have put your heart and endless hours of your time into your business and you've been chastised on the internet for all the world (including your mother-in-law) to see. It can unlock a rollercoaster of emotions – fear, shock, horror, embarrassment, rage, frustration, more rage. Even more rage.

I understand – I have dealt with many an exasperated manager, landlord and restaurant owner over the rocky road of TripAdvisor. But what if I told you that TripAdvisor, or any review site, is a gift that keeps on giving. Would you believe me?

For the next few pages I am going to be using TripAdvisor as my example, but these tactics apply to any of the review sites out there.

The first thing to understand is that these review sites are not really review sites at all; they are social media platforms. Just like your Facebook page, your Twitter profile and your Pinterest boards, your TripAdvisor page showcases what is happening and has happened in your business. It is not an email or messenger service because it is visible for all the world to see, with photographs and reviews available for public consumption. If you search your business name in Google, your TripAdvisor reviews may be one of the top listings.

Because of this, TripAdvisor cannot and must not be ignored. The millions of users it has are not decreasing, they are increasing. Your audience is watching – and waiting; the reviews about your business may get more hits than all your social media pages combined. So you can either pretend this game doesn't exist or you can learn the rules and play to win. And here is how to start.

**Claim your page.** Be sure to claim full administrator rights to your pages. Do not leave this task to one of your team who may in time leave with the only access to your account.

**Fact find.** Take stock of what has happened so far. What are the areas of your business that people love? What are the areas that people are unhappy with?

**Respond to everything.** When someone has taken time out of their day to write something – anything – appreciate that. If a review is negative and has got your blood boiling (it happens to the best of us), wait at least twenty-four hours before responding. Give your side of the story and be responsive without being defensive. Remember that you're not chastising the review's author but educating the thousands of other people who are reading the review and the response. People don't always expect everything to be perfect, but they are interested to know what can go wrong, and more importantly, how the venue responds to it.

There are three main reasons (generally speaking) for a negative review:

**Failure in the experience.** For example, a negative review may concern poor tasting or burnt food, rude staff or dirty toilets.

When there is a failure or breakdown in the experience, it's important to say you got it wrong, this is not what you expect your guests to feel like and you're sorry. This is a great opportunity to show a human side to your business and shine with passion and consideration.

**Failure in the expectations.** For example, the restaurant was small, the music was loud, the drinks were expensive.

When there is a negative review regarding a misjudgement of a guest's expectations, this is actually a great opportunity. There's no need for aggression; the reviewer has invited you to step up and tell the world what you're all about. They misunderstood your style, trend or vision for the business, so be sure to put your side across.

**Your product or service was not good enough.** Reviews are insights into the thoughts of your guests – not always your ideal guest, and they're not always sugar coated.

However, when a reviewer says the product or service needs improvement, you can clearly see what needs immediate attention. What can be worked on? How can you add systems to close the feedback loop and prevent mistakes from happening again?

Which category does your most recent negative review fall into?

When reviews tell you that your expectations need to be realigned, you know what work to do. If people find you expensive, maybe you need a menu on the outside of your building to educate those who are considering coming in. If people find the portions surprisingly small, maybe you need imagery that represents exactly what the dishes look like. If people feel underdressed, maybe film a promotional video which demonstrates the exact look and vibe of your business.

It is not the guests' job to go out and understand everything about your business. You need to have a clear message highlighting exactly what you are, then let them decide if you are the right place for them.

# CUSTOMER RECAP

★ Create experiences that not only satisfy your guests but also surprise and delight them

★ Deliver exceptional experiences to your key guests by having service standards that your tribe know inside out

★ Going the extra mile is what sets you apart as more memorable, and makes your business easier to recommend

★ Online reviews are more popular than ever, so it's essential to understand why people write them and plan how you will deal with them

★ Educate the public so they know what to expect from your business

EXPECTATIONS (+) POSITIVE EXPERIENCES (+) REPUTATION (+) CONSISTENCY (=) CUSTOMERS

**Take Action:** Download the 'CUSTOMER' Workbook via www.joyzarine.com/formula

SECTION FOUR

# CREATIVITY

# CHAPTER 16

# FROM 'BLAND' TO 'BRAND'

*'Innovation distinguishes between a leader and a follower.'*

STEVE JOBS

Being a creative force in hospitality is par for the course. You have to stand out if you are going to be remembered and have a business that survives. This is the step that many businesses rush towards, thinking it is the answer to all their problems.

The reality is, no matter how incredible your cocktails, if you can't get the host to welcome a guest with a smile, you haven't got a five star business. Get the basics right – as right as you think they can be. Once the basics are all present and correct – you have your vision, the culture of your team is strong, and the customers are happy – you can then focus on what makes your hospitality businesses special and develop something to make it remarkable. This is the perfect time to stand up, stand out and get people talking. Be brave, be foolish, but make people remember you.

Having a profitable and successful business is an incredible achievement, no doubt. But how do you ensure that your business is remembered for all the right reasons? How can you build a business that stands out against rising competition and ultimately stands the test of time? How can you take your business from bland to a brand?

Your *branding* sets the tone, style and image of your business; your *brand* is your distinctive, recognisable name. If your brand is strong, your reputation precedes you. People know who you are and what you do before they have even stepped inside your venues.

So why do you need a brand rather than just a business? If you create a successful brand around your business, opening a new site becomes less risky. People will know who you are and what you do. It connects you not only to people who already love your business, but also to people who are convinced they will love your business, based on your brand. Your events and launches will be more exciting; you'll have a waiting list to make a reservation; your business is far more likely to be featured in magazines and newspapers. Industry leaders and influencers will talk about your brand, even championing it to their followers.

Being a brand sets you apart from your competition as an established professional rather than a flash in the pan. Businesses that can build a memorable and recognisable brand about what they do and how they do it ultimately win. If you're the same as everyone else in this crowded world, what's exciting or memorable about that? Not very much. If you're not making a dent, you may end up invisible.

## Be remarkable

Once upon a time in the days of the 'Mad Men', marketing and branding was so powerful it shifted the world. A cup of coffee, a training shoe, a fizzy drink were all ordinary products surrounded by extraordinary marketing that made us brand loyal, maybe even brand obsessed. A turquoise box with a white ribbon from Tiffany's could get a housewife more excited than what was inside it. A cola drink with a bright red label being held by Father Christmas somehow made the product feel magical and connected to the holiday season. Marlboro cigarettes were no more special than the next brand, but the marketing around them made the product extraordinary.

These days, the world does not spin in the same way. People are cautious of the big budget adverts and celebrity endorsements because they know that somewhere down the line they will be the ones paying for them. Instead of an average product with incredible and budget-busting marketing, nowadays people would rather spend their money on an incredible product, inspirational purpose or remarkable experience.

And people feel special if they buy a product that not everyone can have. Mass market just doesn't appeal any more. Blossom Hill may have the biggest marketing budget in the wine industry and fill up shelves and shelves of supermarket space, but if I were buying a gift for a loved one, I think a rare bottle of Grenache would be more special. Craft ales and microbreweries have exploded in popularity in the past five years. Why? Because their uniqueness and the rarity of what they sell means they *feel* special.

Where I live there is a small, unassuming shop front, and inside is a micro real ale house. A chalk board rests in front of the door, stating: '*Real ale only. No spirits. No wines. No lagers. No mobile phones*'. Not much of a welcome – even the handwriting looks grumpy!

But guess what? The ale house doesn't care about me and how I feel. I am nowhere near its target market; in fact, I am probably the absolute opposite of who it wants as a customer. For its ideal customers (of which there seem to be many as the place is always packed), it is a little slice of heaven. The venue is small, so you need to be in early to get a seat. Everyone knows everyone else and they are their own community, coming together to enjoy what they love. To a real ale enthusiast, this place is something special. In fact, it is remarkable.

I did venture inside this micro pub recently to understand more about its appeal and market.

'Only one of these available until next year now,' the brewer told the barman loudly as he made his delivery. Suddenly everyone was up out of their seats and at the bar, keen to catch a taste before that rare beer was all gone. The products are not mass market and have no flashy sponsorship deals with football teams or million pound advertising campaigns; they are local, quirky, made with passion and limited in stock. And this is what has made the microbrewery business a multi-million-pound industry that even the biggest brands in the drinks world are envious of.

Being remarkable is not about silly stunts or quirky gimmicks; it is about being the best in your niche, offering genuine advantages, benefits and a superior experience. This doesn't automatically mean premium or expensive; you could be remarkable for the speed and ease of your service (like Pret a Manger), your affordability (like McDonald's) or your ethical stance (like Chipotle).

## Take the risk

The time to stand up, stand out and be different is now. But for many businesses, this feels scary. I understand. Maybe you'll isolate guests; maybe some will write bad reviews; maybe they'll hate what you do.

Well, I think if you don't upset anyone, you run the risk of being average, unappealing, unexciting and forgettable. That in the hospitality business is *very* risky, believe me.

What makes your business remarkable? It is quite often the case that a hospitality business will be serving an identical product as its competitors. A Jack Daniels and Coke in a Wetherspoons is identical to one served at the Marriott Hotel up the road. So why would customers choose one place over the other? The price? The atmosphere? The entertainment? The service? There needs to be a good reason.

I visit a restaurant regularly that has its own unique style and service (and probably the best roast dinner I have ever eaten). Stepping into this restaurant is like stepping back in time. The furniture, the artwork, the red velvet curtains are all probably more than fifty years old. There are red linen tablecloths, fresh carnations on every table, and the waitresses use a pen and paper to take down your orders. There are no high-tech iPads or till systems here. The decor has, I guess, not been updated in decades – and that doesn't matter one bit.

What is remarkable about it is the food it serves alongside the service it provides. On a Sunday, the host charms each and every table, welcoming everyone as if they are old friends. He spends time explaining the decadent home-made desserts on the specials boards, telling guests he was up at dawn making them with his own chubby hands (his words, not mine) and describing them with such passion and dedication you can't help but wanting to try them all. His wife waits on the tables and his parents are a regular presence around the restaurant as well.

The charm of this family-run independent is in its owners' dedication to their traditions, not bowing to any modern pressure to change. You feel like you are being welcomed into their home as a well-loved member of the family whom they haven't seen in years. It is packed to the rafters, week in and week out, and I hope with all my heart that it will continue for decades to come. It is unique in so many ways and loved by so many guests because the character and old school charm of the business make it remarkable.

If you only ever sell the same products as everyone else in the same way as everyone else, there is nothing for anyone to get excited about. Nothing to feel passionate about. Nothing to love. OK, there may be nothing to hate, but nothing to love? We all need something to love in a restaurant or hotel or pub.

If you do something remarkable, even shocking, in your business, yes, some people will hate it. But if you make your ideal guests – the key people you are targeting – get excited and love you, while all the rest hate you, then OK. As long as there are enough people who do love you, then that's better than OK – it is exceptional. You will have a business that your people – your team, your tribe – will talk about, get excited about and tell everyone about.

# CHAPTER 17

# FINDING YOUR UNICORN

> *'Passion is one great force that unleashes creativity, because if you're passionate about something, then you're more willing to take risks.'*
>
> YO-YO MA

In the hospitality business, we are not just selling plates of food or pints of beer. Instead, we sell atmospheres, experiences and memories.

There are two factors to making our businesses extraordinary: what we do and how we do it. We have explored at length the service side of your business, the 'how we do it', but now I want to look at the 'what we do'. Finding the unique product or trend for your business to set you apart from the competition and help you create fame for your brand – finding your 'unicorn' – can be a game-changer.

We know people don't visit our businesses just to be fed and watered. They could do that at home or somewhere far cheaper, right? What the guest wants is something to love, somewhere special or something unusual to make their experience exceptional. So what makes exceptional? How can you discover the unicorn in your business that people don't necessarily need, but they cannot help but want?

Great modern restaurant Burger & Lobster serves two things – yes, burgers and lobsters. Their unicorn is that there are no menus, no complicated orders, little wastage, leading to queues of people who love the affordable luxury of a lobster combined with a high-end burger.

Finding a unicorn, or a 'unique selling point' as some popular business manuals call it, in the hospitality industry can take a lot of blood, sweat and tears. But you don't need to cut down your menu to just two items or put all your staff on roller skates. The Bellini cocktail, created in Harry's Bar in 1940s Venice, Italy, is now a worldwide classic, and the bar today is still famous for it. One incredible drink, created nearly a century ago – that is one special unicorn.

Being creative and unique in your business is not simply about finding what would excite your guest, but ultimately what excites you too. As the leader of your business, stand proudly in front of your team to embrace new ideas and opportunities. Gourmet burgers may be all the rage in your sector, but if you are a staunch vegan, you would probably struggle to get behind them as a concept.

Now I am not suggesting you only build a business based on your tastes. Many business owners have scuppered themselves by believing they are their own target market – you may not be. But *believe* in the offering of your business and the direction you are taking it in. Remember, authenticity has the power to move mountains – stay true to you.

When your exceptional eventually becomes so good, very good, always good, you need to be aware of this. Exceptional will eventually become everyday. It may take ten months or ten years, but when someone else comes along and stands out as exceptional, you may be left behind. The stronger your business, the more extraordinary your brand, the more likely it is that you will still be on top in ten years' time.

I remember when Starbucks first came to my neighbourhood, in the suburbs of South East London. It was incredible. We felt special – Starbucks had picked us to serve and we were so happy about it. My friends and I arranged to meet up and 'go to Starbucks', and we weren't the only ones. Lines stretched out of the door, with everyone so excited to try a cup of coffee that they knew would taste good. The cafés and greasy spoons in the town felt the pinch; things were changing. Now we felt part of a big city movement that was Starbucks. Cappuccinos had never been frothier and caramel lattes had never tasted sweeter. We loved it – it felt remarkable, and so did we.

Fast forward a few years and going to Starbucks doesn't quite feel as extraordinary any more. Being exceptional is not eternal; the long lines don't last for ever. There are now many more coffee shops around, and though Starbucks's coffee is one of my favourites, it is an everyday rather than extraordinary product.

So what does Starbucks do? Accept that it is ordinary and everyday? No, it works hard to create excitement around its products. Its staff get creative with pumpkin spiced lattes, blended iced Frappuccinos, iced shaken black tea lemonade. It doesn't have to advertise its cappuccinos any more; instead, it has a wider range of new products, but is still working hard to be exceptional, continuing to be extraordinary.

To be incredible and exceptional forever will take continuous effort. Pretty soon, even the happiest waitress or the finest espresso can change from exceptional to everyday – without actually changing itself at all. The properties of the product may stay the same, but the emotion and feeling we have towards it can change.

So how can your business stand out? What product or service style will set you apart? What will build your brand? What will ignite your key guests and your tribe to really believe in it?

Ask yourself these questions:

- ★ What product or service is your business currently known for?
- ★ What is your business never going to be famous for?
- ★ What could your business be known for in the future?

# CHAPTER 18

# BECOMING THE TALK OF THE TOWN

> *'There is only one thing in life worse than being talked about, and that is not being talked about.'*
>
> OSCAR WILDE

When you make the conscious shift to stand up and stand out, people will talk. They will get excited and will spread the word to those around them. If your brand is something completely revolutionary, they will probably keep telling people until it stops sounding exceptional and becomes everyday.

Last year I headed to the famous restaurant Dans Le Noir to 'dine in the dark'. I had read a magazine article about the restaurant and instantly booked up for a table, despite a three-month wait on the reservations list. The day had finally come around and my friend and I sampled the unique dining experience, where you are essentially blind for the duration of your stay. When I say blind, I mean it – you literally cannot see anything. The waiting staff are, in actual fact, blind themselves, the room is completely black, and you cannot even see the food you are eating. You simply decide from a meat, fish or vegetarian menu and food is brought to you for you to enjoy.

It is an incredible, petrifying and invigorating experience, having your sense of sight taken away. It becomes a challenge to navigate food into your mouth, let alone work out what it is you are actually eating. It is probably one of the strangest meals I have ever eaten, not because of the food, drinks or service, but the experience of being blind and everyone around me being blind too. Bizarre, unusual, exceptional, and definitely remarkable. It is an experience I still talk about months and months after it happened, and I recommend it to anyone who is visiting London for the first time.

So how can your business become talked about in magazines, newspapers and on other people's websites? How can you scale up the conversation from your team and guests to official influencers who will spread your message to hundreds or thousands of people around them?

Let's start by understanding what an influencer is. The traditional answer would probably be a journalist or industry critic. Love them or loathe them, journalists and critics wake up every morning with a direct connection to hundreds, thousands, maybe millions of your ideal customers, which makes them pretty useful, really! People read what they write, and follow their recommendations. When a food critic writes an article stating the decadent Chocolate Glory at The Ivy is the must-try dessert this season, people sit up, listen and reach for their phone to make a reservation. They ultimately feel that they want to be part of something so special when it comes recommended by a high-profile source.

In these digital times, though, it is not just journalists who can make an impact. Bloggers, or 'digital influencers' as they are often called, also have an important part to play.

The power of the blogger has gone from strength to strength in the last decade. What started as an open journal for other people to nose through has become a marketing revolution where the author's interesting opinions and discoveries actually matter. The internet has turned a personal log into public property, potentially reaching millions of people, generating decent earnings for the most popular sites.

The key things to know are that blogs are updated frequently and are an expression of the writer's thoughts, usually about a particular topic. Mummy blogs have proved popular, connecting isolated mothers who are drowning in nappy bags and wet wipes to an influencer who has been there, done it and has something interesting, amusing or inspiring to say about it. For the foodies among us, recipes and beautiful, mouth-watering images can be a big hit.

So why do bloggers matter to your business? Well, if a food blogger who obsesses over pizza places has a following of 5,000 in your city, you may want to invite them to try your latest pizza special. If they love what you do, they will want to try it, talk about it and tell everyone about it. Your tribal drum will get a whole lot louder.

## Influencing the influencer

So what the influencer says, goes, but how can you influence an influencer?

Luckily for us, we live in the digital age, and any influencer with a following can be found on Twitter. Following, connecting and understanding what an influencer writes about, and what certain papers and magazines tend to cover, you can really help align your message with theirs. Some journalists may be all about the events, others the community aspect. Some writers obsess over cocktails, others decor and furniture. Realise their passions by following their newspaper pieces, blogs and tweets (and perhaps keeping a crafty spreadsheet of this info). Then when you and your business have something important to say, you'll be able to say it to the right people.

Remember, though, that the influencer must align with your target market. Otherwise you will attract an influx of unhappy people who are not in tune with what you are offering. If you can attract the right influencers who are interested in and passionate about what you do, then you are heading for incredibly exciting times.

Of course, not everyone who calls themselves a blogger is in fact an influencer – there are plenty of blaggers out there too. With a bit of detective work, investigating followers, likes, comments and shares, you can easily see who is the real deal. If people are starting out, there is no reason not to work with them; we all start somewhere. But knowing and understanding the relevance and following of an influencer, and putting that into perspective with the perks they receive, you will connect with the right people who can really help to grow your reputation and tribe.

Attracting the right influencers to write a piece about your business is not necessarily a one-time thing. Cementing relationships can be powerful in the long-term. Imagine if you are opening another site, launching a new menu or trying to bolster votes for an up-and-coming award. Long-term relationships with influencers who are at the end of the phone can make these occasions impactful and remarkable for your business.

It is important, though, that you don't just look at influencers as glorified soap boxes that allow you to talk to their followers. Value their opinions, too. Creating and updating their blog is a passion of theirs, but they ultimately believe that their opinion counts, and so do their followers. They see themselves as experts in their field, so respect their opinion and value it if you want their seal of approval.

Inviting influencers to special events can be a great way to begin relationships. Menu tastings, wine tastings, cocktail creation workshops are all opportunities to connect with them. Testing a menu on a variety of influencers and gaining their feedback is invaluable. Not only will you get some ideas before unleashing the menu on the general public, you will also give the influencers a sense that their opinions count and they have helped to contribute rather than just criticise. Once the menu has been finalised, invite them back to a menu launch – imagine the write-up and review they'll give of a menu they helped to create.

When influencers recognise your business as exceptional and tell their tribe, they will reinforce your five star reputation.

When the demand becomes so great you have more reservations, less no-shows, higher spend and more positive reviews, your business will be remarkable.

# CHAPTER 19

# PARTNERSHIPS

> *'Instead of worrying about what you cannot control, shift your energy to what you can create.'*
>
> ROY T. BENNETT

Why do partnerships matter to your business? Well, for many businesses that I work with, partnerships can be the cherry on the cake. They may not form a huge part of your revenue, but they can be a consistent and reliable source of income that can really improve your top-line sales.

So what have partnerships got to do with creativity? I am going to outline some examples below of how partnerships have changed my and my clients' businesses, but they are not a one size fits all solution (unfortunately). You do need to keep your eyes open for opportunities to partner up, and also understand when to say no.

Partnerships need to work for all concerned or they will be very short lived. WIIFM? (What's in it for me?) and WIIFT? (What's in it for them?) need some serious thought, and be prepared to compromise at times. My golden rule is that if you are partnering with someone, your values should be similar if not completely aligned. A five star Argentinian steakhouse partnering with a vegan mums' group is a waste of everyone's time. The steakhouse partnering with a wine club for their monthly night out could work very well, though.

Here are some tried and tested ideas that I have used over the years to form great partnerships that benefit everyone.

**Wine suppliers.** It is rare for anyone in your business to be as knowledgeable and passionate about the product as the wine suppliers and their ambassadors. Partnering with a great supplier and maybe even offering them exclusivity over your wine supply can pay off for all if they put the time and effort into training your team to feel confident selling their wine.

If your business has guests who are passionate about wine, why not ask your supplier to host a seasonal wine tasting at your venue? It will give them an opportunity to promote what they do and how they do it, and give you an opportunity to wow your guests with a whole new experience. You'll be able to test out new wines on your key guests and make them feel a part of the decision-making process while giving your supplier an insight into the needs of your business.

**Ales suppliers.** One ale company we partnered with ended up becoming a global brand, but in the beginning we were one of the few pubs happy to stock its creations. I could tell from the guests within our business that the product was really hitting the mark and so we gave the company exclusivity on our ales in return for being allowed to host its newest lines a month before everyone else. The company's representatives jumped at the chance to be our preferred supplier and received huge weekly orders from us, while we welcomed ale enthusiasts from across London who wanted to try the latest casks. Everyone, guest included, was very happy.

Offering new and upcoming brewers the chance to host ale festivals within our business has led to some great partnerships. For weeks, they would be telling their loyal tribes across social media, websites, blogs, etc. about what would be available at the ale fest happening in our pub. Their name was on the tip of our tongue constantly as we encouraged people to try their ale and come to their fest. With very little effort on our part, ale fests became key dates with different companies keen to secure a hosting spot at every opportunity.

**Butchers, bakers and furniture makers.** All suppliers have one common goal: to be seen and heard by more people. The more people who know who they are and what they do, the more likely it is that they will have the opportunity to sell.

Blog takeovers are a great way for this to happen. Now this comes with a warning – if your unicorn involves an outside supplier, I'd advise you not to give the game away. Remember that the world (along with all your competitors) is watching. However, if you use a supplier who can be called upon to write a blog for your website about what they do (and hopefully how well they do it), then ask them. The more eyes you can get on your business, the more you will be known and respected for what you do. These are not times to be humble – tell the world your story, and help your suppliers to tell it too.

**Community.** Being a positive part of the community is everyone's responsibility these days, and I can't tell people enough how important it is for businesses, no matter what size, to play their part. We can all do more to help those around us, and it doesn't need to come at a huge cost to our businesses. With a little effort on all sides, you can form incredible partnerships that go on to make huge impacts within your community, which in turn can generate revenue streams for your business. Great wins all round.

**Schools and colleges.** Local school and colleges are often looking for support from businesses like yours. Meet with school and college liaison officers to understand what they may be looking for in the future. Could your business offer work experience or apprenticeship experience for students? Is there a recruitment or training opportunity for you to take part in?

Colleges and universities that offer catering or hospitality courses can be a great source of local employment for your business. Also, dance and acting academies can have an endless stream of energetic and confident students who could make incredible assets to your front of house team. Sponsoring a prize at a college's annual awards ceremony can showcase your business as one that cares for more than just profits to a room packed full of the proud parents of teenagers. Stand out and stand up for the future. You could end up a winner.

**Charities.** Supporting charities, both large and small, is very close to my heart, and always has been. Working with charities in a business sense has often been successful for all involved.

Understand which charities heavily align with your vision. From sponsoring key events like colour runs or moonlit walks, to having an item on your menu that will raise money every time it is ordered, you can find great ways of communicating your passion to help others.

Often at Christmas I will highlight a special on the menu, and every time that is ordered, we donate £1 to a local charity that feeds the homeless. The business then matches the total made by the end of December. The charity actively promotes the work we do, and everyone who is a part of our business does likewise.

Alternatively, offering your workforce to help make sandwiches for the homeless, hosting a coffee morning for those who are alone, or donating leftover products are great ways to support charities. The more we can help each other, the more opportunity we have to grow. Then we can give even more back. Ultimately, everyone wins.

**Meetup.com** is an online social network that connects people, enabling them to pursue a shared passion together. Meetup groups cover a vast spectrum of weird to wonderful, and I have found they offer endless opportunities to create great partnerships that work well. By simply connecting with the organisers, I have worked with a number of groups from wine enthusiasts and ladies who lunch to singles groups and live music fans. If they love what you can offer, there are epic partnerships waiting to be made.

Don't forget my rules about WIIFM and WIIFT, though. Offers, VIP treatment or exclusive rates may be required – the group needs to feel the benefit too. But if you can find a sweet spot that works for all, then partner away!

One great partnership came via meetup.com to a small independent pub I work with. It had very little budget for luxuries such as photographers, so partnered with a Meetup camera club. The club had exclusive access to the pub one morning every fortnight for a couple of hours. The pub staff dutifully served tea and coffee for members as they sat and learned all about their technical theory. Then when it came to the practical, they would photograph the venue, the food, the drinks, the cheerful staff, etc. to their hearts' content. Suddenly the pub managers had an endless supply of great pictures they could use on their website and social media, and a directory of local photography students who would come and photograph events at very reasonable rates. Everyone was happy, and the partnership still stands today.

There are partnership opportunities worth exploring all around you. Remember to work with partners who support the same beliefs as you or speak to the same key guests, and always look for how you can serve first and gain second. Those partnerships are the ones that will work well for all for years to come.

# CHAPTER 20

# CREATING FAME

> *'Fame is not the glory! Virtue is
> the goal, and fame only a messenger,
> to bring more to the fold.'*
>
> VANNA BONTA

I am not about to reveal how to get chased by paparazzi or appear on the front cover of *Heat* magazine anytime soon. The level of fame I am talking about is getting your name, or your brand name, on the tip of more tongues and staking a claim on your piece of the pie within the industry.

Now that you have (I hope) discovered your unicorn, it is time to tell the world about it and shine a light on exactly what you're famous for.

**Imagery.** In the world of creating fame, image is everything. I am a huge believer in imagery when it comes to showing the world what you do. You need to have great quality professional images of your dishes both online and in the press. If you're nervous about spending the money on a professional photographer, alternatives could be to contact a local photography school and exchange your space and food for some great images. Or ask your beer or wine supplier for some financial support to ensure their products are captured within the images. Whatever you can do to achieve great pictures, do it. The return on investment is undeniable. You may be the best – but your images need to *show* you're the best.

Make your unicorn the leading image of your website, surrounded by other great images that show exactly who you are and what you do. In a world where first impressions count for everything, your images and your website need to work hard to showcase what you love to do and want to be known for.

**Website copy.** Your website is the (digital) window to your world. Along with great images, it needs to have some well thought out words to educate your audience on who you are and what you do. Always include a page 'About Us' where you dive into your 'why' and allow the reader to peek behind the curtain at your vision for the business. What is your passion and how are you delivering it? Remember, people care far more for why you do things than what you actually do.

Also use your website to introduce your team. The people within your business are the heartbeat of it, and shining a light on their passions adds weight to your story and your fame.

**Blogs.** Blogging can feel like a task that never really needs to get done, but when you're trying to speak to the right people rather than just every person, a blog can be a quick fire way of doing that.

Your blog is an extension of your business that is like a lesson from you to the reader. You can inform your audience about new recipes, special events that you're excited about, information about special dietary requirements that you have accommodated or unique cocktail creations. By writing a blog about the things that make your restaurant, bar or hotel unique and successful, you're helping your audience, from loyal fans to first-time perusers, to understand more about who you are as a business. Your blog can get you into their minds and into their hearts before they have even stepped inside your venue.

**Google.** When you search for your business online, what happens? Well hopefully your website and some supporting sites like TripAdvisor or your Facebook page jump right to the top – but then what? In the world of digital media in the 21st century, you are who Google says you are, and that means you need to keep on top of what is being said about you online.

To make sure your website is well ranked on the web's search engines, keep your content updated with great images, copy and links. But there are other ways to win at the Google game. Make sure your G+ page is full of updates about your business, and that will seriously help your Google ranking. Getting features on the blogs and websites of influencers also helps to pack a digital punch, so when someone asks if you can get involved in a project, say yes. Keep an eye out for any rogue reports or negative blogs about your business, too. You may not be searching your business very often, but your ideal audience will be.

**Social media.** Do you really need to worry about social media? In a word – yes! Owning your space on the social media landscape has never been more important. If your business can't be found with a few clicks, doubt creeps into people's minds as to whether or not it exists or is still trading.

Right now as I am writing this book, the social media world feels stronger and louder than ever. Platforms that are just a few years old are being bought and sold for billions, and there is one reason for this – their popularity. Nowadays your social media following is a testament to your status as a business and gives clout to your importance within the industry – tough, but true.

Twitter, Facebook, Snapchat, Pinterest and Instagram (depending on your audience) can all generate a buzz around your business and empower you to influence thousands of people through the content you share. With an engaged audience, you will have someone to listen to what you have to say. You can advertise via all the platforms and lead people to your 'Book Now' button within a few minutes of sharing a link – pretty powerful stuff!

The key to winning at social media is to be relevant to your audience, be authentic to who you are and be consistent in how often you post. It is certainly a marathon rather than a sprint, but when your ideas, images and thoughts become nuggets of gold on your profiles, you'll be incredibly glad you committed to starting, I promise.

**Press and interviews.** Getting featured in magazines and newspapers doesn't need to come at a cost through advertising. When you have the right story to tell and the right contacts to tell it to, PR (public relations) can skyrocket your business's image.

Because newspaper and magazine articles feel like news rather that adverts, they seem unbiased and relevant. When people read about your business in an interesting article portraying what you do in a positive light, your fame rating improves instantly.

There are so many ways to get press coverage (which could fill an entire book), but the key is to have something interesting to say that people are going to want to read. You can easily map out the next twelve months with ideas of newsworthy stories in your business, and sending out press releases every time something is happening is a great way to generate coverage. From expansion or a new menu to an award nomination or a special event that you're hosting, journalists want real news. Getting into good habits and building great relationships with journalists and newspapers is key to remaining in the headlines for all the right reasons.

# CREATIVITY RECAP

★ Create a brand around your business to stand out from the crowd

★ Finding your unicorn will not only excite your guests and your tribe, but will excite you too

★ Working with influencers can connect your business to a far wider audience and reinforce your five star reputation

★ Create partnerships with organisations with complementary products and values so you can forge long-term relationships that can increase top-line sales

★ Create fame for your five star business through marketing avenues such as PR, blogs and social media.

---

INSPIRATION (+) IMPROVEMENTS (+) PARTNERSHIPS (+) FAME

(=) CREATIVITY

---

**Take Action:** Download the 'CREATIVITY' Workbook via www.joyzarine.com/formula

SECTION FIVE

# COMMENDATIONS

# CHAPTER 21

# THE POWER OF AWARDS

> *'In the dust of defeat as well as the laurels of victory there is a glory to be found if one has done his best.'*
>
> ERIC LIDDELL

No matter the size or style of your hospitality business there are many great awards that you can enter. There is a huge variety of industry awards, as well as local and national business awards which open for entries throughout the year. If you become an award-winning business you can attract the best talent to come and work with you, stand out against your competitors, and hopefully impress your key guests.

For any business considering competing for awards, there are pros and cons. Awards require time, energy and sometimes financial investment.

I have been very fortunate to have worked on many award applications that have resulted in a gala dinner, champagne, sweaty palms, applause, an acceptance speech and a cab ride home clutching a glass statue or golden figurine. The world sees the pictures, the news clippings, but let me tell you, so much work goes into becoming a winner.

So why do we do it? Why do we want to win awards anyway?

**To inspire and reward.** The process of entering award competitions does not need to fall on just one set of shoulders – nor should it. By involving your team in the process, you can spark their enthusiasm and interest for more than just the day-to day-running of the business. The process of entering focuses them on understanding not just what they do, but *why* they do it.

If you are able to win an award, there will be an instant boost to morale across your team. We as humans want to feel successful and be part of something that matters. Simply being shortlisted as finalists is an honour, so celebrate it as such. Set it out as a goal for everyone and pull them into the application process with their ideas and their visions for the future.

**To build reputation.** Being an award-winning business sets you apart from the competition, and for regular guests reassures them that they have been making a great choice all this time.

I know from working with big brands that when you can add the words 'recommended by' or 'winner of product of the year', you simply sell more. Brands and businesses that have won awards generate a feeling of trust and value. When you buy their product, you perceive that their success and goodness will become a part of you. For example, if a beauty cream is declared 'product of the year', people rush out to buy it because someone of importance (whoever that may be) has declared that it is a winning product. And who has the time these days to argue with that?

When the high street you're on has restaurants, cafés, pubs and eateries at every turn, there has to be something to raise your business above the rest. In my opinion, winning awards is a sure-fire way to do that. If you're looking for investment from banks or shareholders, awards are a great way of affirming prestige and status, reassuring the decision maker that your business is the right one to back. Being an award winner proves that you're not just good, but serious about what you do.

**To examine our own game.** By going for awards with strategy and forethought, you can take a step back and see the reality of what is happening in your business, assessing your achievements, understanding the areas that need improvement and measuring the feedback from both guests and team members. Putting a magnifying glass over every aspect of your business may not be your priority day to day, but to win an award, you have to go on a fact-finding mission to uncover and shine a light on the brilliant parts or people within it. That could be your levels of customer service, your social media and marketing, your commitment to the local community or perhaps your business acumen.

I am very proud to have helped one client go from a previous 'Worst Pub in London' award, aka the 'Grotty Toilet' award (true story), to being named the National Pub of the Year by *Shortlist* magazine. Another client won a business excellence award for customer service within seven months of opening his restaurant.

There is nothing that inspires, rewards and invigorates an entire team more than an award for their hard work. The experience of hearing your name called out in front of a crowd of hundreds or thousands of fellow (and rival) businesses really is special – your very own Oscar moment, complete with black tie and long-winded speech. Bliss!

Getting the judges' stamp of approval can take some doing, but let's be fair – no one entered the world of hospitality for an easy life, right?

# CHAPTER 22

# BEING IN IT TO WIN IT

> *'Winning isn't everything - but wanting to win is.'*
>
> VINCE LOMBARDI JR.

If you've decided to compete for awards – great decision, after all you have to be in it to win it.

When I tell people that I help businesses win awards, they first of all get a look of excitement in their eyes (wondering if they could one day win an award too), and then an air of scepticism takes over. Do I *really* know the secret of winning awards?

Well, unfortunately I am going to tell you there is no secret. There are some tactics that I always follow, but there is no guarantee of success, and there is certainly no shortcut. All awards and judges have their own guidelines and score cards. But what they're not looking for is simple lip service. You have to make sure your business is brilliant and award-worthy before you can expect to be named as a finalist, which is why this is the last part of the book.

So what is the best way to hear your business name being read out?

**Be strategic.** Don't go for awards that you wouldn't feel incredibly proud to win. There are hundreds of weird and wonderful awards, but they must mean something to you, and (more importantly) your business.

When you are considering an award, look at the previous winners. Would you be proud to have your name in among these businesses? Is the size and scale of the award in line with where your business is at the moment? Look at the title of the awards and review which categories you would like to enter. Which would give you great credibility with your key guests? Which are you good enough to win? When it comes to competing for awards, you can hedge your bets across more than one category, but be sure you can do the work for each one. It may be better to have one incredible entry than two or three rushed and mediocre ones.

Display strategic thinking in deciding on awards. As with everything in your business, your awards are not just about what you have won, but *why* you went for them in the first place.

**Be real.** Make sure that the responses you give when going for an award sound like they have been written by a human being. Many businesses put on a stiff and corporate tone using language that belonged in a 1980s boardroom presentation.

Be human; be yourself; tell real stories from your journey so far. This is not a time to be a faceless corporation; be a business leader of a real team, warts and all.

Admit that things sometimes go wrong, and demonstrate how you deal with that. Get real testimonials from the real people within your business. Don't tell them what to say, and don't edit them – let the truth of your business shine through. Do keep it relevant, though. There are word limits on most applications for a reason – people can have a tendency to waffle. Don't let that be you. Read the questions and write your answers, but all the way through check that you are actually answering the question rather than just blowing your own trumpet.

**Be responsible.** Make sure you know what you're going to be entering and who will be taking ownership of the entry. You need to have input from across the business, but someone needs to lead it who's aware of deadlines and submission rules, etc. Make sure you plan enough time to do the work, and do it really well. Leaving it all to the part-time door host is not the best idea. If you are the person who will be getting up on stage to accept the award, you need to give this time, energy and commitment. Don't enter the same content as the year before – it will be obvious. Be fresh and re-energised with every entry you make, and tell *your* story.

**Be brave.** Don't be afraid of the big boys. It can be intimidating if you see the line-up of past winners or sponsors of an award, but sharing a nomination alongside the big and bold brands improves your status. It certainly doesn't detract from it. Just being seen and spoken of alongside great businesses, you allow their star quality to rub off a little on you.

Quite often there will be a chance, either within the entry process or at the awards night, to meet other applicants. Use this opportunity to build contacts, network with other businesses and potentially forge partnerships. These people may not only have great advice for you, but also great business leverage. Meeting the general manager of a successful hotel that is constantly fully booked for functions could result in you getting recommended as an alternative. So don't be put off by the big names around you: get in, shake hands, and see if you can help each other.

The entire process of winning awards can be a journey of self-discovery for both you and your business. Holding a lens over your business challenges you to look at what you do from a new perspective, and that can be very powerful. Think back to Section 1. What was hanging in your hall of shame? How has this been rectified? What work still needs to be done?

When a question or topic highlights a sore point that you just want to steer well away from – don't. Instead, lean into it and explore a little deeper. Maybe it is your online reviews, lack of press coverage, staff retention or training. If there are failings in some areas of your business let these spur you on to create an action plan to be better in the future. This can even be submitted to the judges – speak of your excitement at having created a plan for improvement.

Our businesses are never the complete product with nothing to improve upon. We all have areas we could be better at –

even big businesses like Apple or Microsoft will admit (in a quiet corner) they have a lot more ground to cover and improvements to make. Your business is definitely no different. The best businesses are those that identify not only their strengths but also their weaknesses and how they will tackle them head on.

# CHAPTER 23

# MEET THE JUDGES

*'I think whether you're having setbacks or not, the role of a leader is to always display a winning attitude'.*

COLIN POWELL

You've submitted your entry and you've been named a finalist. Congratulations!

Firstly, by all means, tell the world how happy you are that you have been named a finalist for the awards – tweet it, email it, and add the awards logo to your website. But once that is done, prepare for the next round.

Often after a couple of written entry rounds, you will be invited to meet a panel of judges. You may be invited, as an individual or as a team, to present on a stage or simply talk through your application. Whatever the rules and regulations of the final round are, they shouldn't come as a surprise. Read any correspondence you have been sent or check on the awards website to be sure of what is required and what to expect. No one likes to be asked to give a surprise presentation!

**Evidence.** Be confident that you can prove every claim you make in your submissions or conversations with judges. If you cannot prove it, then reword it as an opinion rather than a cold, hard truth.

Take evidence with you in the form of testimonials, surveys or insights, or analytical documents. Platforms such as TripAdvisor, Google and Facebook have easy to access statistics that can help to prove some of your claims. Your team members are also a great source of information. Get each to write a statement or fill in a survey regarding what it is like to work in your team. Show evidence of your visions, your growth plans and the steps you have taken to implement changes within your business. It is information like this that can set you head and shoulders above your competition.

**Practise your responses.** When it comes to performing well in front of the judges, practice certainly does make perfect. Have a good brainstorm about the kinds of questions they will be asking you and spend time practising your responses. You may have a limited time in front of the judges, so rather than waffling through three or four stories, have the golden one at the forefront of your mind. Record your responses on your phone if you like, and listen back to them. How can you say it better, say it faster, make your point more eloquently?

**Limit the jargon.** Be sure to go through your responses and identify any industry jargon that you may use without consideration. You may be speaking in front of judges who are not familiar with the terms you use in your day-to-day business. You certainly don't want your moment to shine to be lost because the judge is struggling to understand what you are talking about.

If you're in doubt about what sort of language to use, think about how you would describe what you want to say simply and effectively to your grandma. If it is too complicated to write on a napkin, it may just be too complicated, so be sure to break it down into manageable chunks. Be compelling in the stories that you tell, explaining not only what you do, but the reasons why you do it. What problems have you overcome and what challenges have you met that make you the best at what you do?

**Know your numbers.** Check and double-check the information you have submitted, and be sure you understand it. If you have submitted records from your accountants (usually an essential requirement if you're going for a business award), be sure that you understand what they mean. Meet with your accountant to cover any projections and forecasts. You have to be prepared to be quizzed over any information you have submitted, so be sure you understand it enough to speak confidently about it.

**Tell your story.** Nothing matters more within your business than the truth of a compelling human story, whether it is your personal story or one from your employees or guests. Facts and figures are unfortunately somewhat forgettable, especially if the judges are listening to an entire day of interviews or presentations back to back. By telling an interesting story full of passion and delight, you will be memorable and effective in standing out.

Business without the personal element can be flat and boring. You need to ignite the judges by showing them exactly what makes your business, its products and its people special. What do the guests love about what you do? Be sure to bring that to life.

**Winning status guaranteed.** And if you don't win, be proud as punch that you were nominated or named as a finalist. Getting that far makes you a winner anyway – you can still feature the awards logo with the words 'proudly nominated for' or 'proud finalist' across your website, email signature and Twitter bio. This goes a long way to prove your status and quality as a professional and respectable business.

If you don't win, be sure to ask the judges for feedback and take note of what was missing from your application. Pay attention to who did win on the night and start a plan of action for your next turn. It may take more than one attempt, but you need to keep working at it. Winning awards is a skill like everything else.

# CHAPTER 24

# TELLING THE WORLD

> *'It doesn't matter
> how many times you win an award,
> it is always very special.'*
>
> ZINADENE ZADANE

So you have won an award – congratulations! Now what?

This is the time to beat the celebration drum like you have never done before. It is not enough that the few hundred people who were in the room last night saw you win; what about the rest of the world? They need to know too.

**Blogging.** Write a blog before the awards ceremony talking about the excitement and pride that you feel about being nominated and a named finalist. Mention previous winners (especially if they are well-known and prestigious) and celebrate in your own words the feeling of being named alongside such great businesses. Even though you have not yet been named a winner, you have also not been named a loser – you are still in the running. If and when you are named a winner, you can add an update to the blog with the details of your win. What a way to finish the blog post!

**Minute by minute updates.** Nominate one of your team to be the sensible one and do 'of the moment' updates on the night of the awards. Be sure to tweet good luck to other finalists, follow and retweet relevant updates, and build excitement for your followers. If there isn't a hashtag for the night – create one. Take pictures and get excited. This is your moment – you need to own and enjoy it.

Even if you don't win (but you are going to, right?), be sure to be supportive and gracious. By being in a celebratory mood throughout the evening, you will not only feel like a winner and look like a winner, you'll be perceived as a winner.

**Tell the press.** If a magazine or newspaper is associated with the awards, be sure to send a press release the morning after the ceremony. If you are afraid you may have a somewhat fuzzy head, you can always draft one prior to the awards and amend it with details of the event afterwards. Secure some great coverage, and have some beautiful pictures of your latest (and now award-winning) creations on standby so you are all set to bask in the limelight.

If there is not an official press partner of the awards, make sure that you have the contact emails of local press and magazine journalists so you can send the press release and images without the need to turn detective first.

**Update your website.** Now you are an award-winning business, people are going to be curious to find out more.

Make sure your website is up to date with great images and content, and of course a nice, shiny logo of the award you have won. You are about to have plenty of fresh eyes hitting your website, so make sure you are all present and correct – you are a five star business, after all!

**Thank everyone.** And I mean everyone who has been involved in making your business an award winning one. Send a newsletter or e-mailer and write social media updates thanking not just your guests, but also your incredible team who have put the hard work in to achieve this award.

If there are stand-out individuals who have directly made a difference, be sure to tell them just how grateful you are. Create thank-you cards and write personal thank-yous to each and every staff member, supplier and tradesperson who helps in the delivery and maintenance of your business. Make sure every guest who comes into the business is told about the win – add it to the menu and create thank-you cards as bill/ receipt holders.

Without the great people and the supportiveness of guests for the business, there would be no award – so be sure that everyone feels warm and fuzzy with the gratitude.

**Celebrate your success.** Get a date in the diary, book it out and celebrate the success with your team. The hard work has to be worth it, even if it means closing for an evening. In fact, this gives you yet another reason to tell the world of your success. Get a big sign made and hang it in the window: *'Tonight we are closed as we are celebrating our win'*.

You have earned it. Please do enjoy it.

CHAPTER 25

# WHAT NEXT?

*'In the end it's about the work,*
*not the award you get for the work'*

LINDA FIORENTINO

I wish I could tell you my work here was done, but the truth is I am not sure it is ever done. Becoming a five star business is not the end of the journey; in fact, it is just the beginning.

Hopefully the changes you have made within your business have left you feeling more confident and able to grow and guide it for the future. It is important, now more than ever, to keep on top of your game, because you're in the place everyone else wants to be. This can be the time that 'success syndrome' strikes and hits your pride (and your wallet) where it hurts.

Success syndrome is a phenomenon that has taken hold of many businesses, and I don't want it to happen to yours. You started your journey with a vision of being successful – a thriving business that the world admires. You've struggled and hustled, and after a lot of time and energy, you've done it. People came and loved what you were doing. They told other people, and they also loved what you were doing. You invited judges to listen to your story, experience your hospitality, and hey presto – they loved it too. The reservations diary filled up day after day and you were turning away more bookings than you could take.

Then a customer comes in who isn't happy and tells you they will never be back. You shrug off their complaint, knowing the phone will soon ring with someone who will fill that gap. A team member deals with another complaint, and they shrug it off too: 'Plenty more where they came from.'

Success syndrome has struck your business without warning. Complaints are on the rise, as are customer discounts and refunds. Reservations begin to slide, along with sales and profits. The regular five star reviews you were so blasé about slip to a few fours, some threes, more twos than you have seen since you opened.

Success syndrome can be recovered from, but it requires immediate action and urgent attention from everyone. Ideally, though, you can simply take heed of this warning and keep the egos and self-admiration in check.

You must always be clear with yourself and everyone around you that without the guest, there really is no business. All the awards on the shelf and the press clippings mean nothing if there is no one to serve, no one to please, no one willing to pay. Success syndrome is a growing pain that can occur within any business – look out for it; it's a dangerous problem to have. Keep the energy high to strive to be better than you were yesterday, and stay ahead of the growing pains.

You may now be at the point where you need more managers, more team members and more guests than you ever have before. It is essential that every person on your team understands the journey you have been on so far to get to the top, and what you must do to stay there. You are still only as good as the smallest details within your business, and it is as important as ever that your values remain true.

Becoming a five star business puts you in a stronger position for investment, growth and sustainability. Don't let profits swamp the importance of people; it is the quickest way to fall from favour with the tribe who have always known and loved what you do. Be sure that you *never* stop striving to be the best. Keep entering awards; keep winning awards. It will never be easier to be on top than when you are already on top.

Be mindful that over the months and years, your key guests may change. Your customers may have problems, different requirements, new expectations. Your offering may need updating, tweaking, fine-tuning – or perhaps your offering will become so famous that changing anything will shock your tribe to its very core. There are restaurants that have had the same menu for over twenty-five years. That is all they will ever offer, and they are proud of it. Many of us, though, have to keep an eye on what we do and how we do it, and continuously improve it. Your reviews will guide you to the thoughts of your guests (or at least the vocal ones). Never be so self-assured that you stop listening.

# COMMENDATIONS RECAP

★Winning commendations and awards for your business not only rewards hard work, but can motivate and inspire your tribe and rank you above your competition

★Approach nominations with strategy, bravery and honesty

★When meeting the judges, practice makes perfect

★When you have won an award or commendation – get ready to tell the world

★ Keep success syndrome away by continuous examination of what you and your tribe do.

**Take Action:** Download the 'COMMENDATIONS' Workbook via www.joyzarine.com/formula

# AFTERWORD

Now that you have a five star business, be sure to keep the momentum going. Having a five star business is not like climbing a mountain, where once you reach the summit, the hard work is done. It is more like keeping fit. You need to keep running, keep tweaking, keep improving, keep getting better. Be clear on your vision for the future, and be committed to your mission today.

Guests will expect five star service from you and your team, and you must deliver that every single time. How can you do this? Invest in the growth of your team, because ultimately this will result in the growth of your business. By setting your team members' goals and being mindful of their progress, you give your business the best chance of continuing what you've started. Treat your team as well as you want them to treat your guests and set the standard for the future of your business, no matter the size.

Look for great people in your team and ask them what they love to do. Aligning their passions with the needs of your business can change everything. You can't teach passion or talent, so if you find either within your tribe, make sure you put it to great use.

What does being the leader of a five star business mean to you? Your leadership must be rock solid – there will be tough decisions to make, but continue to have clarity in the direction your business is moving in and trust your instinct. If the vision isn't big enough now, expand your dreams. Your options are open and the future for you and your business is bright.

I am excited to hear about your next steps, so please let me know your successes. I am as always cheering you on from afar.

**Take Action:** Download all resources at
www.joyzarine.com/formula

# ACKNOWLEDGMENTS

Tony Adams, I am eternally grateful for your belief in who I am and what I have to say. Over the years, your loyalty has been unwavering, and I would not be where I am without your friendship and (sometimes brutal) honesty. You are the best at what you do, and I feel very lucky to be on your team.

Nancy Richardson and Richard Carr, thank you for being my ultimate dream team. You will always have my gratitude for believing I could do this. I could not have done it without you.

To the legends Emma Mills and Gary Das, my thanks for keeping me on track. When it comes to world domination, I couldn't ask for better partners in crime.

To the wonderful Caroline Sumners, Liz Riley, Paul Giles, Melissa Talago, Mark Huntley, Rosa Kaftan and Polly Ferguson. You have all played your part in cheering me on, I am eternally grateful.

Gareth Marsh and all the Marriott family, thank you for your support in business and in writing this book. I am so excited for your next chapter.

Thanks to my publishers Lucy McCarraher and Joe Gregory for all your wise words, guidance and advice. Daniel Priestley, thank you for your daily inspiration and for creating a dent in my world that I never want to get fixed.

To my mother and all my wonderful family across the world, thank you for always inspiring me to reach for the stars. To my father, thank you for raising me to see the magic in people, and to my brother, Andy, thank you for demonstrating that it's nice to be important, but it's more important to be nice. Love you always.

# ABOUT THE AUTHOR

Joy Zarine is a hospitality and marketing consultant from London, UK. For over fifteen years she has worked with industry leaders to create and market profitable and award-winning brands. From humble bartending beginnings in her teens, Joy has gone on to help launch UK-wide brands and create her own marketing consultancy to support hospitality businesses, especially cocktail bars, gastro pubs and restaurants.

Her passion lies in making incredible and memorable guest experiences, both online and in person, for her clients' businesses. She enjoys helping her clients to create raving fans, happier teams and to win awards. In 2017, Joy launched her online training portal Raise the Bar Academy to empower businesses to stand up, stand out and be more profitable.

*The Five Star Formula* is Joy's first book; she is currently writing her second book, *The Voice of Experience*, which is scheduled to be released in Autumn 2018.

### CONNECT WITH JOY
Twitter: @JoyZarine
Facebook: Facebook.com/joyzarineltd
www.joyzarine.com
www.raisethebar.academy